South Korean author KIM HYUN debuted as a poet in 2009 when his five poems including "Blow Job" were featured in the quarterly *Jakka Segye*. Since then, Kim has published poetry and essay collections and co-authored a feminist novel collection, a queer novel collection and a young-adult queer anthology. Kim has received the Shin Dong-yup Prize for Literature and Kim Jun-seong Literary Award.

SUHYUN J. AHN is a PhD candidate studying East Asian philosophy. When he is not researching, he translates Korean poetry. His works have appeared the award-winning documentary, *Time to Read Poems*. Until 2020, he was the founder and the editor-in-chief of *Nabillera: Contemporary Korean Literature*.

By day, ARCHANA MADHAVAN is a technical writer helping people to make data-driven decisions. By night, she is a fitful writer and a budding translator of Korean literature and comics. Her translations have appeared in *Chogwa Zine* and *Nabillera*, and her creative non-fiction has appeared in *Bitter Melon Poetry*.

THE PRIDE LIST

EDITED BY SANDIP ROY AND BISHAN SAMADDAR

The Pride List presents works of queer literature to the world.
An eclectic collection of books of queer stories, biographies,
histories, thoughts, ideas, experiences and explorations,
the Pride List does not focus on any specific region,
nor on any specific genre, but celebrates the great diversity
of LGBTQ+ lives across countries, languages, centuries and
identities, with the conviction that queer pride comes from its
unabashed expression.

KIM HYUN
GLORY HOLE

Translated by
Suhyun J. Ahn
and
Archana Madhavan

Seagull
BOOKS

LONDON NEW YORK CALCUTTA

Seagull Books, 2022

Glory Hole (글로리홀)

© 2014 by Kim Hyun

First published in Korea by Moonji Publishing Co., Ltd.

All rights reserved.

First published in English translation by Seagull Books, 2022

English translation © Shuhyun J. Ahn and Archana Madhavan

ISBN 978 0 8574 2 987 2

British Library Cataloguing-in-Publication Data

A catalogue record for this book is available from the British Library

Typeset by Seagull Books, Calcutta, India

Printed and bound in the USA by Integrated Books International

Contents

Translator's Note

In the spring of 2018, I got an email from Bishan Samaddar, an editor at Seagull Books. The publisher was curating the Pride List, and he had come across Kim Hyun's poems featured in *Nabillera: Contemporary Korean Literature*, a Korean literary-translation magazine I was running at the time. I gratefully accepted the offer, but then anxiety loomed. How do I even translate Kim's collection? His poems are not graceful. Nor do they incite vivid imagery. He hoards real and fictive references, distorts them, and plays with the violent incoherence that emerges from it. Notes are provided but only to disorient the readers further. (It is important to note here that the notes ascribed to the 'Translator' are by the author himself.) However, this shattering of the sensible world is where Kim's aesthetics lie. It is where queer people in South Korea live and persist. Therefore, Archana and I had to resist the constant urge to render the poems idiomatic, intelligible, and beautiful. Our goal was to emulate the discomfort Korean readers feel when they read Kim's poetry. If readers of this translation ever feel lost, I recommend reading the commentary in the last part of the anthology.

Before I end, I want to thank Mr. Kim Hyun for entrusting his works to us. I am also grateful to Archana Madhavan, a talented co-translator who made this translation possible. And last and but not least, I am indebted to Bishan Samaddar and Seagull Books for their generous support, patience and opportunity.

Suhyun J. Ahn
March 2021

Preface

Death is near this world

To me, love is near

Kim Hyun
Summer 2014

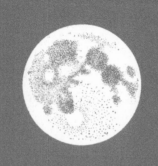

Light is truth

Having drifted, the night returns. A ragged human steps into a dark, crawling tub. From the tip of the human toe that touches water for the first time, fish scales break out in the shade of mugwort. The human, for the first time in a while, is soaked in the slimy sensation.

Fins are more suitable for humans than two legs.

The human repeats. Perching on a bed, the human elongates his neck. Scouting around the meal that several can share, the stretched neck and head sweep swollen dust and glide into a bathroom. The flowing face follows the human fin. The human takes a breath and holds it with his gills.

You've lost human breath, Human.

The human's face radiates like pewter. The nape of the human neck is torn in the shade of lead. A fading little human comes to the tearing human and sits. As he unevenly cuts his growing tongue, the little human, for a change, tries to invent words that a human cannot comprehend.

A human needn't speak human words!

The stretched human wriggles, the disappearing human tongues stutter, the mutated human moves much more naturally, and they are at rest. The tub water's surface is pushed into the night's slumber.

The altitude of the returned night delves deep like a construction crane. Humans separately discover their lives. Humans separately hang out as humans do. Human words that are absent from the human have no meaning. Humans are quiet. They are silent. A ghost that's on strike enters the house without a shadow and illuminates the labor of a candle. Human, human, human disappears like a period mark.

NOTES

1) From humans, a night has emerged.
2) Tonight, the rally of humans makes the poet take the lead.
3) Night humans chant a disabled slogan: "We also want to become humans."
4) A novelist, from a human perspective, writes a poem titled "A Human about a Night."
5) Into the night of humans who have lost a human, a sack of ghosts is walking as though it will be blown away.

The night's interior was dim and cold. After finishing his shift, Michael stormed into his home; he was in a hurry. He lay his body down on a worn couch. He opened a bottle of cheap whiskey. He swallowed billowing darkness. The clear, fishy smell of a chicken-processing factory climbed over Michael's body. Michael dry-heaved as though his bones would break.

Gabriel was lying prostrate on a stain-soaked rug. With a cigarette in his front paw, he was mapping out a place called the World of Cats.[2] Michael pulled down the zip that was fastened to the top. His dark gunmetal coveralls were split into two in front of his empty chest. Black drops of blood fell apart.

Gabriel, when Michael called his name, Gabriel ditched the cigarette and jumped onto the couch. The keen luster of his fur splashed. Gabriel put together his front paws and arched his back. On his contours shone slim moonlight. Michael patted Gabriel's light. The sensation of darkness buried under his soft fur was barren like his backbone.

Michael emptied the rest of the sixth pale lager, Bird. Flying high, Gabriel moved his tail and closed Michael's eyes, which were tattered and out of focus. *Gabriel, I must have been a skeleton ever since I was in an angel's belly.* Michael jerked his muscles. A flock of chickens, with their heads chopped off, fluttered and drifted in Michael's deserted dream. Out the window, bleached feathers fell like clusters of flowers. The carol of children who are blue no matter what formed white frost on the window. Michael's hand, which had once caressed Gabriel, melted. It was a white hand washed by blood.

Gabriel licked a sleeping Michael. Every nook and cranny of Michael glistened. The sound of red high heels came up the stairs.[3] *Purr.* Gabriel cradled Michael's night that only had its frame left.

NOTES

1) In the basement of velvet, pale blue sang, "Patricia, Patricia, Patricia." Then he ended up hiding for a long time. Another song had been made.

2) This refers to the entire feline family. Cats were originally tame clouds, and their major sources of food are night, rain, and snowflakes. Because their eyes can see clearly in the dark, they enjoy reading and contemplating in the middle of the night. They can effortlessly hide or reveal their nails. Ink cats, a type of night-sky cats, are born with wings. Recently, a cat was born with wings in Tianqing, China, which became a trending topic.

3) "Certain inspiration can never escape the moment from which it arises. When I was singing this song, I heard another song from outside. So I thought I should pile up that song with this song and, at the same time, separate that song from this song. Therefore, that song was a part that made up the entirety of this song and simultaneously had to be a red high heel where a snowflake melted into a round water drop; the night that a high heel had penetrated with the click-clack sound; thin and long fingers that grabbed carefully onto a handrail; the entirety of yet another night where a drag queen appeared with a running blue eyeliner." From "An Interview with the Author" in the Tolerance Movement magazine *Eyes*.

Hey there, Cowboy! Run to me with your huge, erect penis. I'm even ready to take out my false teeth.

*

After finishing ejaculation for the eighth time, Lone Wood gave a frail sigh while calming his weary mind. It was his last shoot on the film. Lone Wood slung a Big Man duffle bag, which had been open for a long time, over his shoulder. He was planning to sneak out of the movie set and go to Heaven. He opened the door and went up the stairs. He heard the nibbling voice of red-haired Chichi. Though the sweetness was mostly lost, her voice was still cheap and luscious. Befitting her fame when she filmed *KO Ranch*[1] in her heyday, she transmitted chlamydia trachomatis[2] to a movie set. Lone Wood, still as death, realized that there was no chance of going to Heaven.

*

As the party was at its peak, the drunk homo Dave Cummings shouted. *I should take a look at his monumental dick before I die. Get his foul temper triggered right now. Lonely people, only lonely people would understand my feeling tonight. Only lonely people would understand that this feeling is wrong.* Homo Dave Cummings, whose hand was covered with dark red dots, hummed Roy Orbison's[3] song with his eyes closed.

*

Lone Wood stood before a sink and massaged his Vaseline penis.[4] He spat on it. He rubbed the glans. He tickled underneath his balls. Lone Wood's hand was busy, but the sleeping penis, intoxicated with drugs and indulged by alcohol, did not wake up. Whenever he pulled down the wrinkled foreskin, the foul smell rose. Lone Wood grinned and lifted his head. He stared at an old man reflected in the mirror.   Lone Wood, with a hazy face, wiped away the man who sighs heavily. He turned the tap. The sound of water dropped. It was a blackout.[5]

*

Humans pushed their way through the dark and floundered in the finale of the party. Fallen asleep next to soft Linda, Homo Dave Cummings appeared to be dead. Lone Wood sluggishly came out of the bathroom. Chichi, holding a long candlestick, waved a streak of light at Lone Wood's unseasoned smile. Lone Wood approached Chichi, a small and red lighthouse. Chichi has looked into Lone Wood's pupils for decades. *Of course, Cowboy.* Chichi pulled out her false teeth and followed Lone Wood's bleak bum.

*

Candles were extinguished one by one. The party grew quiet little by little.

NOTES

1) The first ever Western pornographic film to feature the love of a cowboy and a cowgirl. It is known for a scene where the two actors in love watch twilight and discuss existence.

2) Originally, it was a type of germ that causes chlamydia in one's genitals. However, in a pornographic context, the word refers to the healthy, vigorous energy of an actress.

3) A singer-songwriter from Planet 9. He received love from numberless earthlings with his songs that carry everyday emotions. Though he has signature songs like "Only the Lonely," "Crying," "In Dreams," "Oh, Pretty Woman," he might have wanted—right before his death from heart failure—people to remember his unwritten songs like "Heaven" and "ChiChi."

4) This refers to a penis enlarged with Vaseline in it. In the pornography industry, penises are rated according to their lengths and inserted substances, such as Vaseline, paraffin, silicone, etc. A penis that is longer than 33 centimeters without any inserted substance (e.g. Dirk Diggler's penis) is rated A++.

5) "From then on, the light didn't come on for a long time. The Great Blackout had started. All sorts of things happened on the night of the Great Blackout, but I will save that story for later. Because this day of ours has to be entrusted to his retirement party. Anyway, it was a blackout." See "Legendary Pornographic Movie Big Man 2" in *Johnsons*, an adult magazine for boys.

Sam Bill woke up shivering and tightly hugged narrow Eve, who was deep into feeble sleep.[2)] He looked out of the window. The train that had left at eight o'clock was entering the Ghost Forest star cluster, where the dreams of dead birds had grown in a heap. Head tilted, Sam Bill tried hard to recall the time he had spent alone. The cold steam from the train brushed past the leaves of Twinkletwinkle-littlestarhowIwonderwhatyouare and formed into the droplets of dreams. Colorful dreams grew transparent as they fluttered, fell, loved, clashed, parted and burst. While watching the dreams disappear in place of vanished memories, Sam Bill swiftly sank. Eve stirred. Sam kissed Eve on her forehead. Eve furrowed her brows with kindness. *The Sam Bills who have survived—who would they be greeting now?* Sam Bill pondered. Pointlessly, Eve opened her eyes. Eve raised her arms to stretch her body, then put them down languidly. Sam Bill looked into Eve's pupils. With whites having disappeared, the two small and beautiful blackholes looked like the origin of extinguishment. The whistle blew. *Coo-coo-coo, coo-coo-coo*, the sound was doleful. Eve pressed her palms on the window. The tail of the train vehemently beat the bush and escaped. A flock of six-colored Stonewall birds soared all together like protesters. Blind Eve noticed a rainbow feather that flew and clung to the car window. She knocked on it here and there. Sam Bill pulled Eve's parched hand and put it on his chest. Lowering his head, he breathed into Eve's hair. Silence stretched linearly. *It's cold snow!* Eve whispered with all her might before long. Sam Bill raised his head. White grains of stars made out of frigid particles nimbly scattered. *It's a graveyard at the winter beach.* Sam Bill remembered that neither he nor Eve had seen snow for real. Sam Bill pressed his lips to Eve's ear and whispered a mantra.

The whirlwind of white sand they had eyed for various lengths of time grew violent. The train demurely approached the core of the tomb. Unlike his expectation, the pattern of death that countless glass tubes had gained from drifting was more beautiful than not. Sam Bill carefully looked down at Eve's heavy face that was sinking with drowsiness. *We knew the start and the end. It was a relief.* Sam Bill took Eve deep into his arms and automatically closed his eyes. The last song of an android peacefully filled the train. When the train plowed through the dark and crossed the galaxy, each and every android stopped operating. A simulation of the space funeral was shut off. The moonlit night became yet more moonlit. Sam Bill, who was waiting until the funeral was over, pressed the G-button and opened the gate of Earth.[3] Carrying expired androids, the Pigeon raced to the burning Earth with all its might. Sam Bill alone bade farewell to all Sam Bills and Eves.

NOTES

1) The first-generation funeral train developed for a space funeral of humans by the Maetel Corporation. It was by and large called "the Pigeon" because

the train cars were modeled after a pigeon's body without a head and feet. Its whistle also resembled a pigeon sound.

2) At a non-concurring time, he meets David Bowie, who has returned from his recent visit to the Time of the Earth. For a long time, he will not talk about his son's movie that he watched there, where he lived as a singer. The names of the following people were cast from the movie Bowie talked about.

3) A massive crematorium for discarding androids. It goes by different names, depending on androids' birth, residence and the planet they emigrated to.

Dad, take out your false teeth now. My dad said in a colorless tone, *I'm still hungry. You need to go and die. You marked it on your calendar.* My dad colorlessly looked at the red circle. *No way, already? Dad, open your mouth.* My dad's question was colorless. *But Son, why don't you ever raise an objection to the law that deliberately kills a person?*[1] He talked serenely as he pressed his lips to his artificial ear with a built-in Microsoft hearing aid. He lent his ear to the reply that originated in himself. Out of the window, black smoke went up. Contract workers who were ready to tear down humans were waiting. *Smack,* he shut his artificial eyes with the built-in Microsoft contact lenses. It was a familiar smell that made humans anxious. The appointed time came. He meekly combed the Microsoft artificial hair that had been sticking up. He glanced at the Microsoft ceramic false teeth he had taken out. It was the fruit of the era. He shut his yap. Firmly.[2] I took out a green Zero uniform and (in a refined manner) finished getting ready to leave. I looked out the window. In a Zero uniform, his generation—who would be willingly dragged to the slaughterhouse; who had led the world to shut its mouth again—was waiting for a bus in an orderly line. They were all in the fresh shade of green, so fresh to death. Scientific laborers showcased their improved acting skills. It was about how a human must sacrifice for others. It was an image that put humans on pins and needles. I heard the laborer hollering my father's death (in a refined manner). He gave an envelope to me when I came downstairs. *For Meat Processing.* There was a red stamp on it. The laborer flung open the door. I headed out of my house. I put on a smile that was as appetizing as his in the old days. He smacked his lips and wagged his ass, pulling the underwear over his butt crack. The bus was lurching toward me. I made up my mind to wave at him with kindness and despondency while I stepped away and honked. We, for the first time (in a refined manner), looked back at each other. Nonetheless, the door was already shut in a thick fog.[3]

NOTES

1) When the policy to save the globe (so-called "Globe Renewal Act") came into effect, it became popular to use "colorless" in a sentence. This text was written in accordance to what was in vogue when Microsoft went bankrupt.

2) After the Globe Renewal Act was implemented, Microsoft went broke and dumped its artificial prostheses in the market in order to circulate and sell them. This text mostly reflects the colorless sense of humanity of the particular era.

3) As the era of cloning new technologies fully began, citizens of every country cast doubt on the colorless refinement of the "policy to save the globe" and developed a movement where one uses a parenthesis (in a refined manner). In order to participate in the parenthesis movement, this text was described out loud as a slogan.

Upon returning home, Lee held an old plastic box and remembered what had happened in the chapel in Quito.

Ellerton is soft like a chick, so who knew he'd leave behind two rats like them?

In Baby Lee's room, Lee removed his sweat-soaked shadow, shirt and pants. In front of a full-length mirror, he danced a few shadow-like steps. Again and again he threw hooks at shaggy Lee in striped trunks.

I told you my nipples are big and my belly hair is thick and my peanut butter[1] smells foul.

Lee watched Lee in the mirror and swiftly moved his upper body. He nimbly landed a jab. Repeatedly he switched his left and right feet. Lee's jet-black Mohammed testicles[2] pranced to the rhythm. He pulled down his trunks and wheezed. The door opened. Lee disappeared from the mirror with a noise.

I was one of the thirteen rugby players who penetrated the pudding[3] of a beatgirl.[4]

Loftily standing in the kitchen, Lee pulled a Junky Strike from an icebox and drank it. He took a bite of a seasoned sardine from Margaras Corp. He crunched on it.

I listened to the story of the Hollow Mickey Mouse in Ellerton's peace-
~~*ful hands*[1] *simply because of rotten beer and marijuana.*~~

The taste was unreal. In the deep, narrow cylindrical time on a table, two hamsters stomped on each other's faces and affectionately wrestled. Baby Lee tossed chunks of sliced sardine there. A transparent world in a blender violently went quiet.

I'm not a hamster.

Lee closed the lid. He pressed the button. A small, stocky scream was grounded incoherently. Amicable fur and flesh and bones and blood were muddled with dark brown sardine meat.

You trashy homo.

Lee's red eyes met a pupil that hadn't been smashed. Lee remembered the gaze of Ellerton, who had freckles and curly hair. He mashed the button again. He poured and drank the discolored sardine juice, which no longer contained a pupil.

I'm not a hamster, you trashy homo.

Baby Lee thought of the black Maria statue in the chapel in Quito. Lee became ashamedly tearful in truth. Baby Lee opened the lid of the blender. He returned Mickey Mouses to the plastic Disney

Land that had a card of love. The two went back to their own quarters and quietly fell asleep. Lee decided that this unbelievable silence was due to the foul taste of a seasoned sardine which pervaded his mouth. Soon, Lee's teardrops were stripped bare. Naked, Lee whispered. The story that is always told. The story of Baby Lee, who made it back home.

NOTES

1) It refers to semen ejected in a yellow or jellylike form due to a long ejaculation cycle or a large number of emotions. The word appeared for the first time in William Y. Burroughs's *Queers*, published by Bear Classics in 1985.

2) It refers to exceptionally big and saggy testicles. The word appeared for the first time in William Y. Burroughs's *Barenaked Lunch*, published by Francois Publishing Company in 1959. Because of this word, Burroughs suffered from death threats for dozens of years.

3) A quick way to refer to a sexually appealing girl. It was used for the first time in *Junk*, published by the Confession of a Drug Addict Who Has Not Recovered Publishing Company in 1953. However, it became known to the world only after the song "Beat Girl Rhapsody" by Queers grew wildly famous.

4) Slang that refers to a virgin's hymen. See *Express Dictionary* (Nova, 1964).—Translator*

5) This can be understood as a metaphor for experiencing a miracle or a technique (hand job) where one caresses the other's genitals with hands and calms him or her down.—Translator

---

[* This and other notes ascribed to the 'Translator' are by the author himself.— Suhyun J. Ahn and Archana Madhavan]

February 4

Coover, who resembles Sleeping Beauty Who Woke from Thirst, flowed out to the dark living room and quaffed leftover early morning from last night. The sunny sound of rain plodded toward him. Raising a magic cane and reciting, Coover blazed fog from the fireplace. Coover pushed a finger into the blue silk robe of rain that was approaching him. He caressed his belly button and tightly opened the closed door. It was a clear, rainy night. Coover chastely sat in front of a disappearing typewriter in a clean, naked body. Vivid Baby's Breath burgeoned at the fireplace. Coover put down his magic cane between a time and another time and pressed a "2" that had grown faint.

February 4

MorrisandLeeandQueenBeeandOlaandSuedeandJosephandCarl gathered in the castle in the sleeping woods to commemorate a living writer. He or they closed the door of the open castle and entered. He or they drank early morning and became the castle's enzyme that the writer had constructed for his or their whole life. In the bare courtyard was a flower bud of the mist that was wide open to the belfry. Getting drunk on its scent, he or they pulled out a magic cane bought with a talent of gold and recited. He or they went up the spiral paragraph. Deaths, drenched in a dream and life and drunk on an early morning, sometimes fell from the paragraph like flower petals and died; revived. At a certain point, he or they—who gathered in the soul of the writer positioned at the end of the numerous paragraphs—took off wet blue silk robes and threw them, following the author's intent. He or they ~~speckled blue or their~~ buttocks in a circle. Precum drooled from a clean, naked body. He or they were covered with time. It was bedtime to start a meeting. He or they, in a circle, tolled a bell alone. The leaves of the toll expanded. He or they started the day of sleep-talking.

February 4

It was a clear and rainy morning. Funeral guests gathered at Patrick Coover's penis to commemorate Patrick Coover. They had magic-caneandbookmarkandsensitivelensandhatandtrainstationanddaybreak in their hands. They had bought it (them) with a talent of gold at a gingerbread house. As the penis swung in the wind, the closed castle gate shut and Queen Bee came out. Queen Bee tidied her tangled hair and said, *By the look of it, it's not going to work. A rainstorm is coming down from the belfry. I think it would be unrealistic to go up the spiral steps when we're drunk on daybreak.* He or they wiped the liquid that was trickling down and said, while kissing the magic cane, *So this was made here. Gotta wait until the rainstorm eases up and Baby's Breath blooms. With only a silk robe off, it's quite chilly here. For now, let's eat daybreak together as Coover suggested. Take the bottle.* Queen Bee tossed daybreak to them. Queen Bee put down magic-caneandbookmarkandsensitivelensandhatandtrainstation. He or they got goosebumps and continued sleep-talking again. He treated the drunks, who were drowning in daybreak and a dream all day, more like humans. *This is not it.* Coover pulled the paper from his typewriter, crushed it and tossed it to a fireplace. The paper became mist in a split second. It was a rainy, clear morning. Daydreamers, to commemorate Patrick Coover, were sucked into the Sleeping Beauty Castle of Coover. *Now that we're drunk here, it feels like Coover is writing a story of us, with us.* Impatient, Coover removed his hands from the typewriter and stretched them to the whispering sound or sounds of raindrops. As he felt the warmth of his belly button, his Venice that resembles his short nose lengthened slenderly. He knocked over a magic cane. Coover, closing his eyes properly, looked at the slanted liveliness of night sunlight sweeping past the window. The magic cane that was inflating with the touch of Coover was astounding to him or them. He or they struck the keys of an absent typewriter. Daydreamers silently read the writer and time. Coover watched, without being caught, the transparent typewriter that snaps without his fingers.

February 4

NOTES

Announcement to readers: The next meeting had been prepared by means of Robert Coover's *Magic Cane*, but we could not invite him in person due to several circumstances. It's because right now, on February 4, 1932, Robert Coover is entrusting his readers with a literature lecture for monkeys at Aquarius. Next year, on 4 February 1932, I will ask Robert Coover to deliver a lecture about forthcoming February 4, 1932. At last, Coover unfolded time to commemorate living writers.

◉ Announcement to readers: February 4, until now, has borrowed its format from a television show *February 4, 1932* as it is. Its timeline was indebted to the stories of "Sleeping Beauty," "Spanking the Maid," "Pinocchio in Venice," respectively. Therefore, please turn and turn back the clock hands according to each February 4. At last, Coover opened time to commemorate living readers.

With the Dead Ones[1]

Mr. and Mrs. Smith sat on the sofa, and each held a take-out noodle box with the face of a Chinese chef Jackie Chang on it.[2] Smith opened a can of beer. Smith turned on the TV. The news was starting. Smith and Smith slurped dinner, exuding the smell of soy sauce. Smith let out a lukewarm burp. To light up their house that was darkened with the scent of dry soy sauce, Smith flicked a switch. Like a terrorist, the can Smith crushed occupied the first page of the *New York Last Times*.[3] Smith wound and unwound and wound and unwound languid time that was clinging to dark scarlet wool. Smith rubbed his bloodshot eyes. Smith yawned until the uvula was in sight. The news and its title appeared. Smith farted to the signal. Smith too farted five times in a row. Smith and Smith smelled it and laughed face to face. A soggy newspaper folded in half rested on the sofa's footrest, and the tightly-wound wool sat on the edge of the sofa. Between the newspaper and the skein, Smith and Smith were seated motionless like still-life objects. The news came to Smith and Smith once again. Two buildings were collapsing in the breaking story. Smith and Smith bent their upper bodies and escaped the picture. A huge flame rushed out of the crumbling buildings. Smith and Smith rested their chins in their hands at the same time. A scream shot up. The pupils of Smith and Smith dilated. A firefighter crawled out of the building, embracing a girl on fire. Smith and Smith were getting more and more excited. Smith and Smith grinned with the vigor of death. And smoke, smoke, smoke. A black-and-white spectacle passed them. Reality would be perpetually extended. Smith turned off the self-assured TV. Smith and Smith stroked each other's dead genitals once. For tonight's shift, Smith and Smith went into their respective rooms with cheap gin. Mr. and Mrs. Smith, whose traces had disappeared, were fixed as they were in a dark tube.

NOTES

1) As a reality TV show that was immensely popular at this period of time, the cast had to find humans among ghosts while re-enacting all sorts of incidents and accidents.

2) A pornographic film from Brangelina Corp. that bears no relation to the movie directed by Alfred Hitchcock and starring Gene Raymond and Robert Montgomery. It is mainly about how Mr. and Mrs. Smith, who became ghosts, gather in a group with twenty-four other Mr. and Mrs. Smiths in a deserted house for twenty-four hours.

3) Issued in New York, it is representative of the ghost newspapers in the United States. The newspaper usually features ghost gossip.

Write the Novel, the Novel; "Please Find My Shoes. ~~They're Sandals, Blue Sandals~~" by Madame Novel Cabbage*

Madame Cabbage shouted softly as a part of the plan for those who have fallen asleep. *Please find my shoes. They're sandals, blue sandals.* The voice was virtuous yet miserly. Amid the sweating and frowning slumbers that it pushed aside, the voice of Madame Cabbage was limited by birth. Madame Cabbage shook awake a still-young lad who was standing close, face-to-face with her. It was a utilitarian idea. Inside a loose, gigantic overcoat, the lad was right in the middle of aging into the face of a reactionary. The lad tightly closed his eyes. People and this station snapped their heads back and forth at this station. Life steered its way to a transfer station. Madame Cabbage thought of things that became the entirety of our lives in the old days. *If we gather five forces, landfirewindwatermind,* but Madame Cabbage swallowed her loud cry once again. *Let's be quiet. I should talk quietly. We've learned etiquette. We've incurred whippings. Please find my shoes. They're sandals, blue sandals,* and the door opened. Following the people who were shoved out smartly, Madame Cabbage tumbled out of the door. Madame Cabbage stood in front of the door where the transfer was over. Finally, *Please Find My Shoes. They're Sandals, Blue Sandals by Madame Cabbage* unveiled its insignificant splendor along with several copies of free newspapers. Educationally, she stood vacant. The door closed. Crushed by a dream, Madame Cabbage wore an odd pair of sandals on her bare feet. It was shriveled. Madame Cabbage read *Please Find My Shoes. They're Sandals, Blue Sandals*, which was written in shorthand in a rush-hour dream. It was judged. While contemplating individually again, the crowd swayed left and right with their arms folded for the greatest happiness of the greatest number, which they had pursued. It was a posture that had been privatized. Life started to pick up speed again like the motion to impeach. On a day like this, please find my shoes. They're sandals, blue sandals; Madame Cabbage, who had lost blue sandals, missed a station where she had to leave them and leave.*

NOTES

* This fiction is a reconstruction of the entire "Write the Novel, the Novel, Please Find My Shoes. They're Sandals, Blue Sandals by Madame Novel Cabbage," non-fiction of Laura Henry.

* This fiction has different elements from nonfiction's fiction. In Laura Henry's "Write the Novel, the Novel, Please Find My Shoes. They're Sandals, Blue Sandals by Madame Novel Cabbage," Madame Cabbage fails to escape from her life. This is because, to begin with, she does not have a station to get off. She is riding a circulating life, and she finally becomes a part of a sleeping life.

Nine Years on Jupiter[1]

Time slowly approaches me,
who had lived on this land once upon a time,
and once again, I am waiting for a galaxy express bus late at night
The waiting room of this star,[2] composed of the two roots of
    chunky tears,
catches its breath
calmly as it shakes off the leaves of water drops
Please don't leave me
Signboards of yellow and red petals are gradually turned off
and the thick fog shutter door rolls down like somniloquy
The night without you is so desolate,
The doleful song of revolution continues in the universe
Machines with rusty love doze with persistent, forlorn looks as
    they clang
and, toward your dimples,
I become transparent all at once
I let the last bird[3] fly to the pitch-black mouth
The pulp of a raging blizzard is splendidly injected into the sky
Two expunged spiral spaceships are formed in silence
like your two frugal ears
is sadness no longer useful?
Into the tears[4] that are concavely inflated

whether it is revolution or art

a soul that couldn't overcome your barbed-wire fence splashes
    and falls apart

Scientifically, a galaxy express bus will not come

In ancient and even more ancient time,

~~you are trying to head for somewhere~~

A poetry collection of the Earth unfolds like the seasons and

it lands softly on the snowflakes among the tears' blood vessels,
    on the inner eyelids of an underlined sentence.

When would I, too, return?

Water-drop reindeers, gathered in silence, make their clean cones
    shine and *chow chow* . . . [5]

Little by little, they become tainted following the asylum of the mind.

NOTES

1) Special thanks to Sweetpea.

2) The biggest and heaviest tears in our solar system grow on this planet. The area of a forest on this planet is 1,400 times that of the Earth. When the wind blows, water drops rotate rapidly as they fall, and this causes blue stripes on the surface of the planet. The region where hot air rises appears bright, while the region where cold air descends appears dark. A giant purple Mongolian spot on the surface is the biggest lacrimal point in our solar system.

3) A type of medicine that began to be used for a soul in ancient Egypt. There are two types of medicine, "Ka" and "Ba," and they represent a bird and ego, respectively. Powdered medicine Ka has a remedial effect known as "when a person dies, the soul escapes from the flesh and drifts freely"; liquid medicine Ba has a remedial effect known as "even when a person dies the soul stays perpendicularly in the flesh." When one takes Ka and

Ba simultaneously, one has an effect called "Akh," in which one feels like the soul is substituting the flesh for once.

4) A complete view of this concave tear can be found in Ryul's photo album *Terminal* (Ru, 1886)

5) "It originally refers to Chow Chow, a type of a dog from the Moon. Nonetheless, because the Chow Chow's doleful howls toward the Moon sound just like the cry of a departing couple, it is used in place of 'farewell.'" See Ryul, *The History of Farewell* (Ru, 1886).

Blow Job[1]

Blow jobs are a specialty of Grandpa Andy, who turned ninety-nine this year. In the lower part of the town, everyone knows that Grandpa Andy can let semen out in a minute, even when his penis is junked up. Of course, no one knows how beautifully Grandpa Andy sings in Lambert Park—the song he chants with his burst lips after being battered by shit-looking Americans; the song he sings in spangle pants with mermaids, waving a white handkerchief.[2] I clearly remember that night. The night when I crowned bedwetter Duchamp's penis with red lipstick while hiding in a wooden boat; the night when black birds dropped their beaks and soared into the air as they shook off the green shawl of Marilyn trees. With Duchamp, I listened to Grandpa Andy's song that was as enchanting as Mommy's silk-satin dress. In the emerald sky through the window of the wooden boat, a mirror ball spun and spun. And finally, the morning dawned again in Lambert Park when Duchamp pissed recklessly and came out of the back of the wooden boat, shaking his hips. It was I who found Grandpa Andy's corpse with a Budweiser shoved up his asshole. I am a quick boy of Lambert Park. I gave myself the nickname after finishing off the priest Roberto's dick, which smelled like a musty cobweb, in a minute. My original name is Andy, Andy Warhol. It was Mommy, once called Punch Drunk Munroe, who came up with this. It's disgustingly out of style, and I know it too. In 1963. I'm going to record the face of a man[3] whose dick is getting sucked by five beautiful young lads[4] and make it into a movie. And the night when I turn ninety-nine, I will die in Lambert Park.

NOTES

1) A thirty-minute film Andy Warhol directed in 1963. The film only shows the face of a man who is receiving a blow job (Willard Mass).—Writer

2) A slang word from the D'Alembert region. It refers to male-to-female crossdressers.—Translator

3) I, a quick boy, made up my mind. I will hire an actor who looks like monk Willard.—Writer who wrote in accordance with the narrator's note

4) I don't know if it's okay for me to say this on behalf of the writer, but according to me, the quick boy, blow jobs are the exclusive property of men.—Narrator

A Tribute to a Replicant about Which Gary Mumbled[1]

Slinging the saddest guitar in the world over his shoulder Adam said composedly

"He lived a life renewed for the sixtieth time Cause of death is still unknown"

It was at the Costa Del Sol Hotel on the planet S–Pain

You come back with the saddest guitar in the world slung over your shoulder[2]

He was manufactured for the first time in Bel Faust in Ireland which belonged to an Earth from long ago He became a toy for a child Until the child by the name of Gary played "Always Gonna Love You" he selflessly died and was reborn again Until the child as a boy severed ties with his family and left home he renewed his don't-send-me-away life eighteen times in total

You come back with the saddest guitar in the world slung over your shoulder[3]

His life and death were useless in a childless home The program that had codified children was harrowing for childless parents

The child's parents kicked him out and abandoned him blowing on hands and feet that had lost their nurturing He left home and lived on abandoned like trivial things

You come back with the saddest guitar in the world slung over your shoulder [4]

After leaving home he made his official debut as a guitar in the rock band Ski Road Strangely he would blend in with the desolate Black laborers Drunkenly he went through Thin Lizzy and the grief of losing his home was acknowledged

You come back with the saddest guitar in the world slung over your shoulder [5]

As he began to support himself his soul took its own course His life took on the blues and in a split second his nostalgia became famous for its death He swiftly remembered a Boeing plane that had been shot down by a Soviet fighter jet which belonged to an Earth from long ago

You come back with the saddest guitar in the world slung over your shoulder [6]

When he who had meandered back to the Earth in his sixtieth life met the man who looked just like him on the planet S—Pain where the time had elapsed he and he were no longer boys following the wind Full of hope they were calling their lives which Gary had mumbled about "Still Got the Blues" They often silently serenely calmly every so often sipped their drinks

You come back with the saddest guitar in the world slung over your shoulder[7)]

It was a long time a long long time ago but I'm still depressed when I think of you Every day comes and goes but I can't forget this one thing Those plastered with your scent of Scotch sang an advertisement song like adults They said they had performed the song together when they were little

You come back with the saddest guitar in the world slung over your shoulder[8)]

He said he wants to stop dying and stop living and return home He whispered to him If I disappear and you return home the first thing I want you to do is to not remember me They finally blacked out

You come back with the saddest guitar in the world slung over your shoulder[9)]

Slinging the saddest guitar in the world over his shoulder Adam forgot to keep talking in a composed manner

He went back home By now "Still Got the Blues" would've become his and only his He is finally alone until his death

It was at the Costa Del Sol Hotel on the planet S–Pain where one minute has just ticked by

NOTES

1) Since then, a new bioethics law ensured there would be only one clone per object. However, the Coalition of Bioethics, which opposes cloning, still insists on a total ban on the production of cloned objects. They suggest an increased production of robotic lives, including humans, as an alternative.

2) This is a rock-band-style notation of "Skid Row," a death code entered by clones when they renew their lives. It is known to have codified a part of *Blues for Isuguro*, depicting individuals who miraculously survive an airplane being shot down.

3) This is from a song "The Saddest Guy in the World," which brings together in harmony "Blues for Isuguro," and "Skid Row," a song often sung to pay tribute and a folk song of the USSR, respectively.

4) After overcoming many obstacles, I uncovered a line of verse that had lost its way from the end of the title track with the same name as the album *Blues for Isuguro*, which was released in xx70 by the rock band Ski Road.

5) As I noticed them, I introduced sounds that repeatedly go on and off when *Isuguro for the Blues* plays backwards. *Isuguro for the Blues* was the first ever code-name for the airplane shootdown that happened on Earth, and the name of an album released by Ski Drow in 19xx.

6) One part of the graffiti left by Costa del Sol at the hotel he stayed in on S–Pain. Later, Costa del Sol composed a song tribute by adding this graffiti to a Soviet Union folk song.

7) The punchline of a sixty-minute commercial featuring the rock band Ski Road, for Isuguro, a company that only specializes in producing whisky. With this advertisement, the sales of Isuguro Scotch skyrocketed.

8) I wrote down some of the soundless verses from "USSR," a song by the blues band Scotch Whisky, which gained popularity throughout the universe for the line inscribed on the ticket of Galaxy Expressway, which heads to Ski Road on S–Pain, via Isuguro and Costa Del Sol.

9) Out of *Blues Code–Ski Road*, I brought and adapted the reverse side of a parenthetical sentence as follows: (Gary Moore was a stud who played the guitar in the saddest way.)

As the whereabouts of Greengrass became certain, his shabby neighbors opened their artificial lips, saying that he must have returned to the cemetery of Planet 3. Even after moving to Planet 1, which had started a green business, Greengrass was a man still under the shadow of Planet 3. He recollected the place down to its last detail and hoped once again to be imbued with the glory of his construction days, filled with the smell of dust. That was also why he fell asleep, lying in a flying glass tube where construction songs played automatically on repeat every night.

Knight Rider and Greengrass conducted a final inspection of the surface tension at Four Major Rivers manufacturing plant.[2] He displayed the following old New Euclidean hologram[3] related to the nasty song Greengrass carried around in his famous perfume bottle.

In the sky are puffy clouds . . . In the river floats a cruise ship and the happiness that everyone deserves is always . . . The mountains and the fields grow more endearing as we watch them. The ideals of our mind endlessly . . . Whatever we want . . . Whatever we will . . . For this land full of grace, like this we . . . sing.[4]

The heavy mechanical harmony of the twelve moons stopped. Knight Rider, who was frowning and watching the blurry song, hurriedly closed the hologram kit. He left the factory with a shivering tongue. Rust bloomed on Knight Rider's shoulders.

i, the whining cyborg of winding Samgakji, went out with Greengrass every week. i clicked on his own nipples. He played back the whining he had recorded while biting and sucking. Every time i lowered and raised his eyelids, Greengrass's old, innocent voice came from his mouth.

. . . I'd love to build a picturesque, multipurpose building on green Longshan and cement it with you, darling, for hundreds of years.

Shuddering, i tore out the voice-recognition wires popping out of his neck. He cleared his throat and attested, I recommended I'm a Cyborg, But That's Okay Hospital.[5] I heard about Planet 3 Syndrome on Denci Hinji's show.[6] i washed his white breasts and went back to the glass tube.

Greengrass was completely undetected. Following the repaired river, droughts and floods broke out. Planet 1 gained a file extension called "tomb." People quickly forgot the whereabouts of Greengrass. Their forgetfulness unfolded in stride. All of the planet's water weeds shattered. The twelve giant artificial pump moons that produce the rivers waned and lagged behind. The demolished building, machine, and humans came blackly into view. Some people changed based on what they saw and, like freedom fighters in solidarity, put Greengrass in the refrain of the song Green Grass.[7] Greengrass, who was dreaming the graveyard, became the symptom of the tomb.

Greengrass who disappeared appeared shortly after all the production facilities that had accomplished the cemetery moved to Planet 6. Greengrass opened his eyes in the flying glass tube which turned into an opaque state of insomnia again. Greengrass lifted the lid of the tube and walked out. Abandoned tubes floated in the sky like commemorative-ad balloons, and a wrecked casino ship floated on the parched riverbed. Greengrass administered a great quantity of artificial tears, which everyone deserves. Assured that he was back at the graveyard he had yearned for, he quietly pulled out the first-generation hologram and, in a dusty voice, and sang.

O, our fatherland,
O, I shall love thee forever.

NOTES

1) Verse added to the chorus of "Green Grass" and sung by the electric girl living in the tomb.

2) In the year XX10, the first production facility began its operation on Planet 3, where four rivers had disappeared, however, as the planet turned into a cemetery, all production facilities moved to Planet 1.

3) A second-generation hologram based on Euclidean geometry which can vividly re-enact three-dimensional figures. Nowadays, the sixth-generation hologram Neutrogena is often used, as it can vividly manifest the emotional state of three-dimensional figures.

4) One of the many popular songs that was widely sung during the green project on Planet 3. Later, it was remade on the various newly constructed planets. This is borrowed from one of the many versions sung on Planet 3.

5) A shadow-removal hospital that was built in the place of an ex-world psychiatric hospital. It is known for removing all kinds of shadows, like visible

shadows, invisible shadows, floating shadows, submerged shadows, thick shadows, thin shadows, etc.

6) *Do Androids Dream of Cemeteries?* is a radio program hosted by Denci Hinji (an electric girl), a sci-fi novelist and folk musician suffering from story amnesia.

7) A song sung widely during the last stage of Planet 1 during which moisture had evaporated. The song was transmitted to Planet 1 by moonlight, the cemetery's public frequency. Depending on the feelings of the machine singing this song, different words or sentences were added to the chorus.

The Moon's Lips [2]

The Dingbat Dingbat women of the Mongolian highlands, having swung from the calves of the wind since their youth, are often mistaken for men due to their rock-hard spirit and crude eyes, but who cares.

In the evening, the mother midwives of the village bare their breasts, colored scarlet with the poop of red twilight spiders, and climb atop the wild donkey Dinga Dinga to seek out women who are almost due.

Anyone who comes across the mother midwives at night kisses their ripe breasts that droop! and wishes their dead sisters long and healthy lives, for they believe their sisters in the netherworld will bless them with a healthy child.

The Dingbat Dingbat people call these mother midwives the Moon's Lips.

The Balls of Macho the Libertine [3]

Known as the Rooms of Giant Breasts for their ability to yield enough milk to soak the labia majora of prairie buffaloes, the mother midwives of Pampas are descendants of their sister gauchos, who subdued the stiff weapons that had invaded their grasslands and defended their smooth ridges for hundreds of years.

This is a fact that only those who do not know do not know.

They ride freely on horseback and roll cigarettes and keep knives and bolas hidden in their long leather boots; and shaking their giant breasts, they chop off the balls of Macho the Libertine now and then and throw them to the crows for a snack.

The young brides of Pampas crush dried crow poop and smear it on their cheating husbands' pillows.

Aleut Village, No. Aurora [4]

In an Aleut Village in Alaska, where it is believed that an ember and a grandmother's song can melt the heart of a frozen person, there are baby midwives called the Story of Beginnings.

Over the long, long night drawn out by a pale blue blizzard's eyelashes descending to the ground, Story of Beginnings, rubbing the new mothers' eyebrows and cutting a path, name little wanderers after old songs.

Below the wind's swim bladder as it crosses the Aleutian Range and under the moon wearing a hat of sweeping clouds, reindeer antlers dance and pluck stars with wild wolves wearing snowflakes.

At #Aurora of the Aleut village, there is a green tundra where a fresh story sprouts each time a child's name is called anew.

Bachelor Ghosts' Nighttime Walk [5]

Grandma Wolsun is a ninety-nine-year-old maiden from the Under-the-Moon village, which formed when the moon fell on its buttocks, and who retired from the world of midwives after falling in love with the wind and snow many years ago.

Even in recent days, her strong, black hair grows every morning because she has wondrous fun every night with a young messenger of death who visits her, for he mistakes the drooping eye she has from a stroke for a wink.

And so the old midwives who gather in the moonlit cemetery and play cards are not captivated by a good hand, but by the night-time entertainment hosted by Wolsun with the young messengers of death.

In the middle of the night, as the moon throbs, to the occasional sounds of the skins hitting, the village widows retch unwarranted and some give birth effortlessly.

This is also when the bachelor ghosts who live alone in their tombs take longer walks at night.

NOTES

1) Last winter, Mr. Neruda—who worked as a mailman on the island of infamies, from which stories were not to be removed—smuggled out the following ten stories, hidden between pages 1,000 and 1,001 of the first edition of Borges's *A Universal History of Infamy*, and of which an excerpt has been translated—while avoiding the saliva-dampened fingers of the quarantine officers.

2) Once upon a time, when there were two moons in the sky, people called the period during which the two separated moons slowly overlapped a "kiss." Lovers made love during that long kiss, and this love was called a "kiss."

3) According to the recipe that the older sisters from the wind-crow family studied for hundreds of years, the most delicious testicles—which is known to everyone who would know—are the testicles of a playboy. And

one of the most delicious ways to cook the testicles is to stir-fry them with
pig testicles and two spoonfuls of pig urine.

4) The following is the longest name in Kachatkam under the moon, where
young widows live together: "One day, a ninety-nine-year-old young widow
came to see the midwife and said, 'Look, please give my little wanderer
who will be born soon the longest name comparable to Kim Suhanmu-
turtle-and-crane-180,000-years-old-Dong-Bangsak-chichikapo-sarisari-
senta-woriwori-seberukang.'"

5) The night was wide and deep, so virgin ghosts got together in the do-or-
die construction site [. . .] (I could not record the words because they
were stained and illegible) gathered [. . . (stains) . . .] all kinds of men
and roasted them and simmered them and fried them and ate them, and
there were virgin ghosts whose bones matched those of the bachelor
ghosts taking a nighttime walk, living side by side for hundreds of years.

Cobweb Carpet

We are like the spider
We weave our life and
Then move along in it
We are like the dreamer who dreams
This is true for the entire universe

The Upanishads

Mr. Raju Handique, living in life, weaved a sparkling carpet by plucking out a transparent dream every night. At daybreak, human-faces gathered under the carpet and drip-dropped water. Asshole! Asshole! Asshole! The legs trembled lightly. Tremors spread to spiderfaces below. Whether it was Raju Handique's dream, carpet, or story, the spiderfaces called it "Asshole Arabian Nights" and passed it on and on.[1]

✳

Raju Handique the Rickshaw Driver is a man who eats spiders. He eats spider-leg soup, spider-abdomen curry, spider sambar, and chapati, parota and puri with spiders on top. He also eats spider sashimi when he has no appetite. I don't know if it tastes good (if you're curious, try! try! try! it yourself). Spider-eating Raju Handique is a story from one thousand nights ago. You have to go back in time[2] to understand him.

❋

That night, a drunkard knocked on Raju Handique's innermost window. It was Mr. Raju Handique. Give me a drink that never makes me drunk even if I drink it again and again, and I'll let you weave a cobweb carpet. Raju Handique took out a dream he cherished. About the time his dream was almost gone, the eyebrows of the sky were erased. Falling asleep to reality, Raju Handique exclaimed, Eat more or less cobwe and b! b! b! Watching his son stay up all night with his dream, Raju Handique's mother said, I'm worried you'll turn into a real spider after eating them day and night, but it's not a big deal. A single cobweb carpet can pull you out of life's honey bucket.[3] The dream has begun.

❋

That night, two crescent moons in the shape of eyebrows adjusted the space between them.[4]

The lady followed her nanny to moonbathe, and her face, which is ugly for the first time in the village, was hung in Raju Handique's dream.

Nanny,

Lady, confronting the light of Raju Handique, passed out lickety-split on the spot.

Lady! Lady! My ugly lady!

When will she open her eyes again?

Faces around the lady worried about her.

She had black moss on her face. They worried.

Her stiff hair was sprouting from her nostrils. They died worrying about it.

The hairs fell and stuck fast to the piglets.

Spring came with four feet at first, then two, and then three at the last.

When she opened her eyes, the lady was the oldest girl in town.

✳

Raju Handique ran into a starlight mystery in the middle of the night. She sank down into fate. "Nanny," the girl closed her eyes in a flash. Raju Handique weaved the girl every night. The face became dreamy. In order to find the face, Raju Handique hung the face over the window sill. The faces passing by the face cried out. *No fair! No fair! No fair!*[5] Blind years went by. The faces that were trying to take the girl's face did not show up. Raju Handique's mother starved to death in life's honey bucket. Raju Handique was barely withered and twisted. The sky turned yellow irregularly. It turned blue. It was a night when the two yellow and blue Moons that look like eyebrows widened the space between them. The naturally beautiful daughter of the daughter who resembled her naturally beautiful nanny said, I will bring that face in. Raju Handique serenely followed the naturally beautiful daughter of the daughter who resembled her naturally beautiful nanny (to be continued).

NOTES

1) According to the story told, a part of Raju Handique's last carpet is preserved in the cobweb southwest of life.

2) A time travel that can often be seen in life. It usually utilizes an organism's sleeping force.

3) A derogatory term for the toilet alley, where excrement buckets are abundantly buried, in the southwest region of life.

4) When there were two moons in the sky, people simultaneously dreamed two dreams each night. People called them a "human dream" and a "spider dream," respectively. Once and only once a year, these two dreams overlapped, permeated, and spread, and people called this period "the night when the two moons that look like eyebrows adjusted the space between them."

5) One of the what-in-the-world exclamations used by the rickshaw drivers in the southwest region of life. The expression spread throughout life as Raju Handique's comedy-tragedy *No, Fair* became a big hit.

Readers, this is from fifteen days ago. I went out hearing a ghost's gibberish in my sleep, and there, a frozen blonde girl was growing old without a sound. She moved her mouth noiselessly, *Mister, I'm on my way to silence. Can you let me have a sip of words?* For some reason, I wasn't surprised and invited the hunchbacked girl into my mouth and pressed a bowl of words and a berry of adverbs into her hand, telling her to drop by whenever she passes through. The girl, who grew even older in that moment, cried as she departed and said, *Thank you, Mister. I just want to tell you, if a beautiful girl who looks like neither a human nor a ghost comes to you tomorrow at this hour and asks you to lend her words, tell her to go check another house because you ran out. Please, please do so.* While listening to the story of the girl who had aged suddenly, I summoned back my half-gone spirit, and found myself to be asleep. The girl was nowhere to be seen, and the bowl of missing words and the seeds of adverbs were watching me blankly. Suddenly, I recalled a few light words that didn't exist. I fished them out and recited the words that I'd recalled and sailed into the vast sea of sleep. A few moments later, I finished reciting them and opened my eyes. The dreams were gone and the words had stopped existing again, and three and a half days had passed. I was hungry. So I came out of my mouth. I was determined to buy paper and a brush. Come to think of it, that was long ago. I strolled past the salivary glands. To my delight, Lord Nikolai,[2] who had eleven children by different wives and had yet another child in yet another woman's belly; and old man Lai O Ming,[3] who had twelve wives; and Karlos[4] the bachelor, who had tied the knot twice with six wives, had all lost their words and had set out their big bats and were haphazardly wandering around the glands like mute ghosts. At that time, there happened to be a reckless madam[5] among the ghosts, so I opened my mouth, and she grumbled without saying a word. *Look at this person growing old. What's the big deal about a living person losing words?* I've lost my words. It wasn't that I didn't know anything about silence. Silence had been turning over in my mouth for a long time. But no matter how I tried, I couldn't forget the blonde girl or blondie's story, so I bought paper and a brush and aimlessly did whatever, until I ended up writing you a letter, readers. I'd like you to come by any time, it doesn't matter when. Just signal your presence, and I'll comfort the silent ghosts and send them to you as soon as tomorrow night, so please come with them in fifteen nights. Look into their situation on the sly. For the time being, I'll try to make a list of the sunken words. Who knows—this might be the key to solving the case of the missing words.

NOTES

1) This was inspired by Korea's first epistolary detective novel, ____. ____ has no fixed characters, events or backgrounds, so there are many different versions of it. For this reason, I will indicate all the titles as ____ and pass it on to the readers.

2) Nikolai, who starts to appear in ____, is killed by his twelfth wife in ____ and continues wandering as a ghost until he reaches ____.

49

3) Lai O Ming is abandoned by his twelve concubines in ____, but continues to mooch off his twelve legal wives until ____.

4) Karlos, who started disappearing from ____ spent two wedding nights with each of his six wives, but is depicted as an unfortunate figure who has never not been a bachelor, who has survived relentlessly so far without cumming.

5) The reckless madam who disappeared after ____, reappears in ____ as a single woman who lost her two daughters to three village libertines she throws the story into confusion by jumping between detective and criminal, human and ghost. The confusion is still unfailingly passed down to the readers of today.

Mr. Withers of Withering Woods[1]

Alright, you are now entering the withering woods
However this story is not about woods

You enter withering woods and stand somewhere underneath
a shriveled long-necked tree
However this story is not about trees

You enter withering woods and stand underneath a shriveled
long-necked tree and catch unripe windfalls of time with your bare
hands

Now when I say "wild grass," you will become a story that is not
about forests or trees; you will become a song about Mr. Withers in
the withering woods who took a bite out of the poisons of time.

Wild Grass grows thick on Mr. Withers's face[2]

Mr. Withers enters the withering forest That night dead Mr. Withers
goes ahead of Mr. Withers and Mr. Withers tags along with Mr.
Withers while the Milky Way flows with sympathy for the withering
woods SomewhereTwoEyesWideOpen Owl lingeringly weeps and
broods within the inner eyelids of the withering forest The weeping
woods is luxuriously and lushly green Mr. Withers's face is blue to
death Hushed Mr. Withers is slowly hanging the fog that has grown

in chunks Mr. Withers heads to Mr. Withers and he sniffingly circles the night in the withered Withers forest However this song is cannot be seen Mr. Withers finally embraces Mr. Withers and they slowly roll around on the SplitSecond vine of the withering forest Mr. Withers and Mr. Withers stroke each other's eyebrows like new brooms promising each other eternal love Slumber pours from your eyebrows However this song is not about those two Mr. Withers's fog becomes a single DreamingMatildeBlueBabysBreath Submerged within a faint early morning dream Mr. Withers escapes the withering forest He returns alone to his thin dust home In his fog-shrouded pajamas Mr. Withers lies once again in a bed full of thin dust for a split second Mr. Withers rubs his withering eyebrows and whispers in sleep You have such beautiful sleep On Mr. Withers's withered face where wild grass grows thick fog droplets are full of moisture and Mr. Withers shrivels with blue However this is a song that ends with the death of a person

Now when I say "fate" you will open your eyes underneath the shriveled long-neck tree in the withering forest and throw away the time which now has a yellowing bite mark and seal your lips and return alone to your thin and faraway home Mr. Withers you will never remember Mr. Withers of the withering Withers forest where wild grass grows thick.

Mr. Withers has passed away[3]

NOTES

1) When the following hypnosis was taking place—this hypnosis is safely lonesomely taking root in Mr. Noxen of the rusted Noxen forest—I failed

to recall the rusty guitar of Mr. Noxen's, by poet Lee Jenny. Later, I came to think that my hypnosis was similar to Lee Jenny's and that it flipped open perhaps Africa. Mr. Noxen's rusty guitar played in that flipped-open space. From that point onward, my hypnosis had become outdated. And yet, I still decided to make use of that outdated hypnosis to the rusty sound of the rusted guitar played by Mr. Noxen. This is what we call fate. Still, I ~~hope not to inconvenience the poet's fate.~~ All of the single quotation marks that appear from now on are sounds quoted from Mr. Noxen's rusty guitar, and so I verbalize.

2) "Arrrrrrrrrrrrrrrrrrrrrrrrrrrrrrrrrrrrrrrrrrrrrrrrrrrrrrrrrrrrrrgh" A single coincidence flew toward me. From the pupils of that black bird, which I watch from eight-thirty in the morning to six-thirty in the evening, hang the wild grass of director Alain Resnais. In the wild grass is a faceless man and woman. A drawn man in overgrown green wild grass holding a red purse and a drawn woman with overgrown red hair carrying a green bag. An image inevitably wears out as it begins. Therefore, I decide to draw the face of coincidence on Mr. Withers until the end. This is also what we call fate. Yet, I hope not to inconvenience that fateful image. All the single quotation marks that blow in hereafter are quoted leaves picked from the wild grass, and so I shake.

3) "A place where nobody thought something would be born. For example, wild grass sprouts from crevices in the wall or ceiling, the two people who absolutely have no reason to meet, and the two people who have no reason to fall in love are likewise." Alain Resnais says, it's likewise. Lee Jenny and Kim Hyun, Alain Resnais and Kim Yun, and Novalis and Kim Hyun are likewise. He(she) and he(she) are likewise. And foremost, you, who's reading right now, and I, who's being read, are likewise. This is what fate is undoubtedly about. Yet, I bloom the hope of not causing inconvenience to the fate's likewiseness. All of the single quotation marks from now on are the romance extracted from Novalis's blue flower, and so I globalize.

A UFO passed by. Watanabe sat naked on a Western toilet. Several mayflies were calmly asleep, their long ears glued to the bathroom wall. Had the ecstasy and the marinated cat[2] he had eaten in the evening gone stale? Watanabe strained his lower abdomen. Yellow-green drops of urine trickled out. *That's not a bad start*, Watanabe muttered through his blue lips. Through the bathroom window came the shattering sound of an altercation between a grand ideal and a small ideal. Today, once again, the problem was with the small ideal. *You just want to remain a frightened child forever.* A glass bottle thrown by the big ideal, the thick smell[3] of the liquor bottle smashed to pieces, and the sound of the small ideal's song shattered. *Same as always.* Watanabe's low voice echoed through the silence of the bathroom with its mouth sealed. Watanabe trembled looking down at the pubic hair on the toilet, his face blue. Watery stool gushed out of him. Ecstasy is just poop in a honey bucket. Watanabe stood up, blinking eyes that had become tender. He flushed the toilet. *Seems like the shushing sound will swallow me up soon.*[4] Watery waste trickled from between Watanabe's boney legs. *That's basically a green monster. Not a bad end.* Watanabe, who was looking at his tongue in the mirror, opened the cabinet and took a dose of depression and daydream.[5] *I'm just saying I won't get along with this world.* The voice of the small ideal came whining through the window again. Watanabe roughly turned on the cold water and kept his head lowered underneath the influence of the showerhead for a long time. He sank feebly into the water. He buried his melting face between his knees. The green waves streamed like tears toward the sewers. *Watanabe-san, Watanabe-san. We're out of dissociation.*

~~The flash knocked on his heart while pills rained down from the~~ sky.

NOTES

1) "The following ongoing reports of more than 20 unidentified flying objects spotted on Grub Street resulted in a spike in interest. According to an article published in *The Moon* on the 3rd, witnesses saw a row of flying objects in the night sky between 11:30 p.m. and 12 p.m. In particular, most of the witnesses said the flying objects stayed in the air for several minutes and dropped white pills, although the identity of the pill is controversial."—*Drugstore Daily Good Night*. See the release on the 13th.

2) A side dish made using the white meat of wild cats boiled in soy sauce. It was created for the poor working class when the black rat president was in office and is still loved by many to this day.

3) Title of a song released by Belgian singer René Magritte on August 16, 1967. It is included in the album *After Death*, along with songs such as "Golconda," "This Is Not Marijuana," "The Treachery of Images Called Ecstasy," "The Philosophy of Ms. Bedroom, High on Cocaine," "Pyrenees, the Castle of a Drug Dealer," and "The Empire of Lights."

4) Possibly inspired by Madagascar, a large cockroach belonging to the gigantic cockroach family. Also called a "whistling cockroach" due to the hissing, whistle-like noise they make. Known to make noise when they are lonely and communicating with others.—Translator

5) A pill made by non-chemically processing the ash resulting from burning a short story by Edgar Allan Poe. It was released without anyone knowing during the black rat's presidency, but now its production has officially ceased due to a number of positive effects. Not long ago, a file titled "The Ultimate Guide to Producing Depression and Daydream" detailing its manufacturing process was circulated covertly on the Internet.

Nightswimming[1]

The Green Monster Outdoor Pool, where embarrassing midday noises had disappeared, is now owned by Bill, who contained Michael and Mike and Peter. Bill pressed play on the old cassette deck. *It was a big penis-like day.*[2] Mike removed a name tag that read "safety" from his thick neck and flung off his Libido swim briefs. *Linda Lovelace's triangle*[3] *was hot, wasn't it?*[4] Peter answered as he shook his wet hair. Water droplets dribbled from Michael's earlobe. *The moon rose low on the surface of the water today.* Michael yawned and watched the rolling wave moon. *That's your sallow face. It looks like Linda Lovelace's crushed tits. This is an R.E.M.*[5] *song, you idiots,* Bill mumbled at the same time and stopped mopping the tiles covered with scum and moss. The mop stood in silence. *It's time to leave this place.* When snowflakes scattered one by one, Bill began to mop again. *It reminds me of that day. It was near the beginning of September. I'm waiting for the moon. If there were two moons in the sky and I were circling the sun, shining alongside their orbits, I would never be able to describe its intoxicating light. You want to go for a nighttime swim on a quiet night, don't you? On a quiet night. Just shut your mouth.* Mike and Peter pushed Michael into the water. *Hey, you're really horribly tone deaf.* Mike and Peter shouted together, wagging their genially floppy balls. Michael, who had been sinking for a while, pointed his belly button toward the night sky and floated upward. The night sky is most beautiful when you look at it from the water. Mike and Peter flopped down on the shiny tiles and dipped their feet in water. They lifted up their outrageous faces of youth. *We're all grown up. Westwestern Wafers is no longer our home sweet home.* Bill raised his head and intoned quietly. *Those constellations have been beautiful where they are for a long, long time, Mike. Look beyond the universe. The ladies who are spreading their eagle-wing*[6] *are waiting for Peter's baby lotion.*[7] *Michael, we're not stars, we're night. We're the darkness that makes stars stand out the deeper it gets.* The song stopped in the dark. Bill threw the mop at the damned cassette deck. He stopped talking to himself. Bill climbed down the ladder to the empty pool. Time hovered by the blue-tiled outdoor swimming pool. Bill walked to the center that had once been filled with water. *I don't think everyone will understand.* Michael, to the hum of Mike and Peter, started to sing for old Bill. Eyes closed, Bill pressed his head to the dry floor and lay down. He lit a Lucky. A UFO brushed past the moon. Like two moons, unidentified flying snowflakes poured through the smoke. *It doesn't feel like the old days.* Bill sang out, a knowing expression on his face that he was growing old. It was in the middle of the night before closing hours.

NOTES

1) A song from *Automatic for the People*, a nighttime album released by the band R.E.M. at an outdoor swimming pool one minute before its closure. This title was borrowed from that song.

2) Another expression for a bad-hair day.

3) A term referring to a triangular hole formed by a woman's crotch when she is standing with her legs together in tight jeans or a swimsuit.

4) It is unknown whether this, in fact, refers to the actress Linda Lovelace, who starred in the pornographic film *Deep Throat*, or a woman who looks like her.—Translator

5) "R.E.M., which takes its initials from the rapid eye movement that occurs during sleep, was formed in 1980 at the University of Georgia and con-sisted of Michael Stipe (lead vocal), Peter Buck (guitar), and Mike Mills (bass) and Bill Berry (drums). Beginning with *Murmur*, their albums include *Reckoning, Fables of Reconstruction, Life's Rich Pageant, Document, Green, Out of Time, Automatic for the People, Monste* and *New Adventures in Hi-Fi*. After Bill Berry left the group due to health issues, they continued to release albums including *Up, Reveal, Around the Sun, Accelerate,* without adding new members." This note, as such, is worth consulting but not particularly memorable. In this case, "memorable note" refers to one in which Johnny Depp, who is equipped with the component of loneliness, delivered their condolences to me. I wish him happiness with all my heart. The Johnny Depps who'll be coming to you soon.

6) A term referring to two legs opened wide (M) and fully exposing the facial expression of the genitals.

7) A term referring to white, sticky semen that curls up like a sleeping baby.

A UFO landed in Dreamland. It was where the model spaceship had disappeared. There stood a real boy.

—Let's leave Earth.

Last weekend, while drinking white milk, the real boy said to a growing real boy *According to math that should be wrong, on Someday the 13th, a UFO will land somewhere around here.* Someday came. The real boys, whose bones had been stretched bit by bit, packed their backpacks with a calcium heart. Just a little, as little as possible. The real boy mutilated products from Earth, saying they're all useless.

—Let's meet at that hour.

The real boy texted the real boy. He stared at the unresponsive chat window. The real boy's allergic rhinitis malfunctioned. Clear mucus ran from his nose. The UFO's massive light poured onto the small town where everyone was asleep, just as they had intended. The real boys' time was meaninglessly necessary. The real boy was on the verge of unknowing. Snowflakes fluttered, the color of Hockney.

—Are you watching? They're the water drops of the universe.

It was a message from the real boy to the real boy. The real boy put a Voyager 17 spacesuit for enthusiasts, a Leica helmet with a mini camera, and, lastly, *Translated Poems* written by an archeologist into his backpack and zipped it up. It was the kind of night he needed to secretly console himself. The real boy placed *Têtu* and *Buddy* under ~~his mattress. He did not trespass on the dreams of anyone in his~~ family, just as he had planned. He opened and closed Earth's last door to the universe. Tightly tying a dahlia-patterned scarf around his neck, the real boy walked toward the mysterious, massive spray of water, leaving behind the slumbering people and the slumbering house. He recited part of a poem.

When we fall in love for the first time,
All of us are looking toward the stars.

The real boy was gradually enveloped by the night. He lost his way and hence found his way. The real boy passed the rose bushes and entered the deep sea of the night. He sent one last message to the real boy. Over his head, water drops in the shape of ammonite accumulated one by one. The real boy was sinking. *To not escape, just don't think of escaping, said the real boy, as the real boy waited for his response like a girl.* The real boy started to leap over long moments of time to get closer to the amusement park in his dreams.

Last year, at an amusement park, there were traces of a spaceship that had disappeared. The real boys' days ended with the amusement park. One boy, caught between other boys, masturbated and spat out semen and swore and then disappeared.*

NOTES

❋ I write this thinking of the boy who disappeared last year from La Vie en Rose. The boy confessed his love to a boy as they passed by a monument to the revolution. Would it have even been possible? Since then, 2,202 days have passed. An ammonite was found in the rose bushes of La Vie en Rose.

❋ The boy confessed his love to the boy as much as possible. I found an ammonite in the rose bushes. Last year, the small and big amusement parks that disappeared from rose-colored lives numbered 2,202. This created an atmosphere reminiscent of a monument to the revolution.

Long-Tailed Darlin[1]

> Her night grew from the tail.
>
> —from *The Tail End of the Stars*[2]

Dar stood at the door wearing a turquoise house dress with frills under the breast. It was Lin who had recently moved to Sunday Morning Road.[3] The door opened.

Darlin put down a plate of savory walnut cookies on the mahogany table. Darlin's tail was thin and long. Such was the nature of long tails, which no one in this neat little town could ever have.

In sadness, the graceful moonlight poured ever more slowly through the window. Darlin stuck her loosely hanging hair behind her ears. Her thin, white face came clearly into view. It had such a beautiful bone structure. Darlin stroked her tail and maintained a ruffled silence.

When the season for collecting the eye of a storm came, the husband needed to be away from the house for a long time. The husband believed that, of all people, his wife, who was home alone, should have a long tail. His wife's tail never grew, day or night, and the husband came back, carrying a snowstorm on his back. His wife's tail made the husband's heart contract. His wife was beaten, and the snowstorm scattered. His wife was beaten, and the snowstorm scattered. His wife was beaten, and her eyes scattered in the end. An army of red-tomb ants came looking for his blind wife.[4] The husband had a belated premature death. Grow longer tail, tail, grow longer. His wife recites the spell. Tail, tail, grow longer. His wife wants to stay alive only if she has a long tail.

The walnut cookies on the plate revealed their true selves. The ants swarmed. Darlin cleared the cobweb vines and flung open the broken glass window.

A gust of wind whipped through the street with the inelastic closed doors. Dead leaves suspiciously flew up. Sank down. One leaf went up one leaf went down one leaf went up one leaf went down one leaf went up one leaf danced and hid itself until the very end.

Expanding and contracting its ruffles, Darlin's tail passed through the hallway and empty room, and climbed over the window. It flowed down, performing the Sunday-morning tune. The short-shortskylarks that saw Darlin's tail sang in chorus with mysterious skin.[5]

Stretching her body, one woman was coming out of the house one woman got scared out of her wits and one woman screamed. The women's fingers stayed between the woman standing by the window with her long tail hanging down and the woman on the street dragging her long tail along with a grumble.

NOTES

1) Though it didn't begin under the direction of photographer Gregory Crewdson, I did sometimes recall a few of his photographs. I do not elaborate on the notes of some of those photographs as per your quota.

2) Innux's last book of astrology, in which horoscopes, done by connecting the tails of stars vertically and horizontally, were written only for the one dead woman she loved her whole life.

3) "For something, refer to the Velvet Underground's 'Sunday Morning'"— See Gregory's inspiration photobook *Innux*.

4) Somewhere in Jack Crewdson's *Unpaged Encyclopedia*, which I read ninety-nine years ago, I remember the tail sentence went something like—if you want to know the exact sentence, read it yourself—"These ants of the red-tomb ant family have nests distinct from those of other red ants, as they make tomb-shaped nests by spreading dried leaves within the curve of animal or plant skulls."

5) The title of a film directed by Gregg Araki. I hope you apply velvet sound to the following narration from the tail section of the movie. "I wished with all my heart that we could just . . . Leave this world behind. Rise like two angels in the night and magically . . . disappear . . ."

Initially, this animal pierces a hole in its tongue and hunts still-phony Dick Head at the Melancholy Crossroads . . .

Last night, Agyness Deyn attended a party at the Plaza Hotel to read James Salter.* She became drunk. They whipped three ordinary readers with criticism. They smoked marijuana. They pierced their tongues. A comet fell as they were swaggering home. Agyness Deyn halted. She wanted to pick a few blossoms of the star's eyes for McDormand. Agyness Deyn bent down. Seizing the moment, Agyness Deyn's anus opened with whoosh. When her bloated stomach was soothed, Agyness Deyn finally set her massive rear down on the sidewalk. A one kind of happiness blew in. It was a cool breeze from Arlington National Cemetery. The star's eyes set off together on a voyage to the night sky. Agyness Deyn tilted her head and looked up at the pupils that had flown briskly into the sky and were sloshing. Those were her buoyant days, the prime of her life. Hey, you fat pussy. If you didn't rent out Melancholy, just put away that pathetic chunk of flesh. Dick Head's caramel-colored saliva landed right on Agyness Deyn's unparalleled thigh. Dick Head's grin, stretching and dangling, lengthily licked the back of Agyness Deyn's ear as it passed by. Keeping her emotions in check, Agyness Deyn stood up and used the sleeve of her silk blouse, which was missing a button, to wipe off the saliva. Agyness Deyn straightened her legs and chased intently after Dick Head. A half block of the moon was obscured by clouds. In a secret alley, a born-again shadow nonchalantly straightened its shoulders. Agyness Deyn, her shoulders finally squared, sprang out at Dick Head. Agyness Deyn bit down

eyes flowed out lightly. Dick Head kept on screaming and cursing. Agyness Deyn felt a sustainable and bizarre ecstasy. Agyness Deyn extended her fingernails, like the stray cats in Bangkok, and finally tore off Dick Head's ears. Dick Head spread his feet in the air, his hands covering the blood that was pouring out of him like shouts of joy. Agyness Deyn chewed and swallowed a piece of flesh in the shape of a V. *It feels like eating six beef patties all at once.* Agyness Deyn's heart was pounding. Agyness Deyn spat out Dick Head's golden hoop earring. Comets fell *alla marcia.* The Star's eyes blossomed. The sky's iris opened wide. Stray hairs grew twinkling on the nape of Agyness Deyn's neck. Agyness Deyn lowered her body as much as she could and crept back to Dick Head, who was in a frenzy. Suddenly, Agyness Deyn's massive body rose weightlessly in the air.*

NOTES

* American novelist and screenwriter. His works include *The Hunters, Still Such,* and *Light Years.* His short story "Last Night" was made into a short film starring Frances McDormand in 2004.

* Regarding the birth of the film: Last night, at the James Salter reading party at the Plaza hotel, the attendees (including me and McDormand and you all) collected and read the titles of the works James Salter wrote over a period of six to seven years. McDormand, you and I met there for the first time, and "Big Animal" started out as a story you and I heard from McDormand. Of course, McDormand's anecdote was a reconstruction of an incident published in the *New Yorker* and in which McDormand's romantic partner was immersed.

Thus, the case was settled as follows. Father Hölderlin took off the stiff, linen clerical collar and placed it on the altar. Once his constrained neck was free, Father Hölderlin, far more relaxed than before, pulled up his black cassock. Below his red thong, Father Hölderlin's bony legs were exposed. With several festering abscesses, his red butt cheek looked like the cheek of a pubescent boy. Some members of the congregation bit back bursts of laughter, their shoulders heaving. Father Hölderlin put his hands together and started Kyrie.[1] The congregation crossed themselves. Mrs. Thomas[2] sweetly released the leash in her hand. Two Dobermanns sharing one neck approached Father Hölderlin, ears stiff, as if they had been waiting for him. Chubby congregants, too, rose from their seats and followed the Puritan monks. Father Hölderlin's lips reciting the Old Testament were stubbornly closed. The monks' sharp teeth were stuck, point blank, in Father Hölderlin's calves and thighs. Father Hölderlin's groan flowed down. The congregation sprinkled holy water from the altar on Father Hölderlin's rear. As they held the rolled-up whip and made it sparkle, Hallelujah, they whipped Father Hölderlin's rear. Hallelujah, they whipped him ferociously. Hallelujah, they whipped him even more ferociously. Father Hölderlin's skin broke and drops of blood, mixed with holy water, splattered everywhere. Red droplets permeated the monks' black woolen clothes. Eventually, the monks licked the blood off their teeth and turned away. The seated congregation sucked the blood off their fingers with reverence. Mrs. Thomas clutched at the leash and adjusted her face. Father Hölderlin dressed himself again. Face flushed, he said, *Salvation is pain.* The congregation lifted their arms and began singing "Lamb of God." Moonlight permeated through the stained-glass windows. The naked body of little Thomas,[3] who had been crucified on the altar, was dappled in color. Warm urine flowed out from Thomas's dead penis. Mrs. Thomas shouted at the top of her voice. Father Hölderlin knelt down and opened his mouth wide.

NOTES

1) "Kyrie Eleison," a prayer said before "Gloria in Excelsis Deo" during the Penitential Act of the Catholic Mass. It means "Lord, have mercy." When I first heard this prayer at a church, I did not feel anything in particular. But when I heard this prayer at a cathedral, uttered by a young slave gazing ardently at his master's whip, I understood the exact feeling that Kyrie should entail.

2) Mrs. Thomas, who had lost her husband Thomas too early, loved her twelve-year-old son Thomas so much that she named her two-headed dog Thomas and licked Thomas and Thomas with a friendly tongue day in and day out. That is what I heard from Thomas, who I met at a beach in Venice. Therefore, this is not a fact that I know for certain. In fact, the fact is . . .

3) I brought the first impression of the following underline I found at Thomas, *The Great Cathedral* (灣, 1912): "I saw Thomas Mann in my dreams. To be precise, it was a boy with the face of old Thomas Mann. I had met him somewhere, but while I was dreaming, I didn't remember

where. And that's right when the incident occurred. That's when I noticed that the Thomas in my dream was the Thomas from that time. A sorrowful dog staring at Hölderlin's whips at a masked ball in Venice."

Sirius Somewhere[1]

Sirius dropped his underwear. The phallus of Tension Penis Corp[2] made a stiff appearance. Even the four beads under the glans looked just like mine. Had solitude a shape, wouldn't it be just like those beads? At last, I began tearing up my body with the old MacGyver knife that Sirius had handed me. A black-and-red solvent gushed out. My heart raced between the long, cold, never-ending electrical circuits. You too are nothing more than an industrial robot. Sirius's humane voice was altogether mechanical. It was neither resentful nor hateful, but softly affectionate and tender. I lay on the bed with Sirius in my arms. I covered us with a blanket of emotions that have been banned since the twenty-second century.[3] I closed my eyes. Sirius began barking a lullaby to the sound of a peacefully beating heart. *Joie de vivre*, which I never knew as a human, surged through me. But it might also be something stored in Fictions.[4] I couldn't open my eyes. You don't have to force your eyes open. Long-tongued Sirius licked me in a voice that was loving because of his long tongue. Sirius, do you think I have a soul too? Code blue. Code blue. My lips twitched on their own. It seemed like an auto-destruct sequence had been initiated. A Roy Orbison[5] song trickled through the air. *Go to sleep. Everything is alright.*[6] Sirius's heart and mine, through which lubricant leisurely flowed, were explosively calm. Where do you think we'll end up when we die? asked Sirius. I can't forget it. I was reproduced with a double-separated phallus from Tension Penis Corp. for the coming generation. And looking for Sirius somewhere, I've arrived here, on Planet 13, already.[7]

NOTES

1) The Wolf Star, a star known as "wolf in the sky." It is also the name of the first-generation pet robot created by Olaf Sky, the founder of Tension Penis Corp, in collaboration with his lover, Stapledon Wolf.

2) A manufacturing company that started out specializing in fake dildos modeled after animal genitalia and later specialized in pet robots. Their headquarters is located on Planet 486.

3) A blanket manufactured in a lover's discourse. It is made with hair from the descendants of centaurs.

4) A program named after Isaac Borges's book to mock him for first claiming that robots also have souls. The program was so designed as to initiate the auto-destruct sequence if a humane error was detected in the robot.

5) A singer who received more love on Planet 3 than on his home Planet 9. Because he sounded like he was from Planet 9, he met a lonely death at an old age while floating through space in a single-person glass tube.

6) From the song "In Dreams," an arrangement of the song "Sandman," with additional lyrics, which used to be sung in one part of the Colorful Desert on Planet 9.

7) Under the presidency of the black rat, it was forbidden to say or write the names of stars because they would raise left-wing hopes. Today, the galaxy's fugitives call Planet 13 the "Cemetery for Turntables."

Dear Old Miss Lonelyhearts*

of "Dear Old Miss Lonelyhearts"

It was the night of the 12th. I woke up and there was a hole in the left side of my chest. It wasn't a big deal because I knew the night that my heart would vanish would come without warning. I got up from bed with the hole and headed to the bistro with Francis's table. Between one foot and two feet, between window and curtain, the wind whistled through the hole. I felt refreshed. I opened the cabinet sleep where the plates of the dead were kept and the cuckoo chirped. One white plate and one red apple. Thursday passed. I held the plate in my hand and placed the apple into the hole. As a person who bore an apple, I swallowed my saliva. It had some kind of taste. I pushed the apple. The sound of it tumbling out of my back flew out the window with a flutter. I served thoughts of the weight of my soul leaving my body in a plate and put it on the table. I stuffed my body in an overcoat and climbed out the window. My body was light like a gram and I walked on top of the road. When I reached the alley with the fire station whose watch tower had fallen, the clouds spread soft legs. From dark genitals, a bright yellow light trickled down and gathered like dew at the hole. In the cracked pavement, the sundrops pooled like raindrops. I had become a person who gave off light, but I was not comforted. My overcoat straightened itself. I existed carelessly in my ludicrously large, laughable over-coat. I wandered two more blocks like that. I didn't run into anyone. Two blocks were at worst that type of distance. I arrived under the One Million Dollar Fortune at Nathanael West Plaza where candle-light is out. There I met old Miss Lonelyhearts, looking again at the lights that were off. I will make this night yours. Instead of money, he asked for my heart. Oh, no! My overcoat opened itself and showed her the hole. Darkly he opened his lifeless eyes and approached my back. He bent his waist and put his head inside my overcoat. The world I see through you is not much different, she whispered like a midnight cowboy. She put her slender face to my back and rubbed it in. His pale hand neared the hole. I laced my fingers through the sweetly stretched fingers. Her tender pink palm was oh so tender. I lay on top of him and the night grew bright. Wandering the alleys, wandering the night, I wandered back home. When I cross the win-dow where the apple that disappeared lies, Francis Jammes is there, the plates of the dead are there, and the weight of my soul is on top of that plate. I lay down on the bed and put the heart I cut out of old Miss Lonelyhearts into the hole. So, dear old Miss Lonelyhearts, are we not for the time being lonely hearts? A red droplet fell from Miss Lonelyhearts's leather overcoat on the hanger. I heard the sound of church bells that were thoroughly soaked. A dream like the Lord's Prayer gushed out.

—Please respond as soon as possible. Yours Truly, a Regular Reader.*

NOTES

* I am pleased to share that the following title was taken verbatim from "Miss Lonelyhearts's Life Advice" published on Friday the 13th in Nathanael West Company's newspaper, *The Lonesome Newspaper.*

* The following road movie starts at Lonely Hearts and ends at Lonely Hearts. I want to walk with you. I want you to open the door in the direction of dear Old Miss Lonelyhearts of "Dear Old Miss Lonelyhearts" and come out inside. I will set your heart as the appointed showtime.

* I share, darkly, that following painting's motifs first came from *One Million Dollar Fortune* by Miss Lonelyhearts that hangs in Nathanael West Plaza.

* The following story begins from American writer Nathanael West's major work *Miss Lonelyhearts.* This work reflects loss through the eyes of Miss Lonelyhearts, who makes a living by answering the questions of *The Lonesome Newspaper* readers.

* One day while getting advice from dear Miss Lonelyhearts, I asked her, "How many notes would you add to the empty spaces of life?" Then dear Miss Lonelyhearts suspended all six notes. There was no need to reflect, it was lost as I thought. But, pardon me, who am I who is speaking right now?

* Later, this regular reader will send additional letters titled Old Miss Lonelyhearts, Help Me, Help Me; Old Miss Lonelyhearts and the Dead-pan; Old Miss Lonelyhearts and the Lamb; Old Miss Lonelyhearts and the Frozen Tongue; Old Miss Lonelyhearts and the Clean Old Man; Old Miss Lonelyhearts and Mrs. Shrike; Old Miss Lonelyhearts on a Field Education; Old Miss Lonelyhearts in the Dismal Swamp; Old Miss Lonelyhearts in the Country; Old Miss Lonelyhearts Returns; Old Miss Lonelyhearts and the Cripple; Old Miss Lonelyhearts Pays a Visit to Doyle; Old Miss Lonelyhearts Attends a Party; Old Miss Lonelyhearts and the Party Dress; Old Miss Lonelyhearts has a Religious Experience; Old Miss Lonelyhearts

and the Hunter of Lonely Hearts; Old Miss Lonelyhearts Recites Francis Jammes; Old Miss Lonelyhearts Goes Missing; Old Miss Lonelyhearts Forgets Herself; and Old Miss Lonelyhearts Stops Giving Life Advice. However, this regular reader hasn't received a single reply (advice). The reason is simple. They share the same heart in different times.

Old Baby Homo[1]

In an empty summer classroom where purple rain comes, I sucked emotion for the first time. The emotion was murky like when I jammed my soccer cleats while clenching my teeth. Moths of time burgeoned in a white cloud outside the window where I was kneeling.

To the command of a herd of toads that were marching down the wet school yard in single file, my buddy dashed with all his might. I remembered his sparkling dribble. His lips blurted "fuck" every time he scored, and quite magically so. The emotion muddled up with drools was soft and slippery.

Soon it streamed down. Hiding the testicles of emotion, my buddy gave me a dry and lovely kick. It was when I, inside the window, looked at myself like an old bride, having been eaten up by time. He pulled up his pants stained with poop and disappeared and was beautiful and. I whispered like a wedding veil. Goodbye.

And nobody had seen them. Nobody. Yes, nobody.

Why have we, who were wiping Hometown ketchup with a napkin from Uncle's Burger, aged so hastily? The tattered night when we wear a wig with sausage curls and drink fetid beer, I sing unintelligibly. For the sake of the buddies who shot a rocket beyond the boy's orbit before the countdown was over. Goodbye, for the sake of homos'[2] emotions who are at a glory hole[3] with yellow buck teeth; who must be fleeing from purple summer in their crumpled soccer cleats. And cheers.

1) Here are the seasons that lent a hand to this song. The disenchantment of spring, the song of purple summer, h and autumn and h of autumn, and Min, the season that does not exist in this world.1-1)

    1-1) I thought of introducing songs that lent a hand to this note, but I decided to leave them in the dark. Except I've listened to John and Charles and Gregg and Min's "The Origin of Love," "White Puppy Like a Beggar," "The Coach Violates Me," and "When You Were a Boy" . . .

2) This word comes from a Greek prefix meaning "to be alike." In consequence, in many European languages, "homo" still means "to be the same." It is sometimes used as a shortened version of "homosexuality," but since the start of the LGBT rights movement, male homosexuals have been called "gays" and female homosexuals "lesbians."—Translator

3) In place of the public restroom that provided space for the hole, I bleakly draw in pop artist Keith Haring's work *Glory Hole* (1980).

Death

Death began heading toward Earth in 1969.[1] Those who witnessed death's first few steps were bent on cutting off young death's legs. They developed diapers[2] and advertised a team composed entirely of white nannies.[3] A number of incubators[4] were effortlessly birthed into the sky. Deaths one after another vanished without a trace. Living organisms that can or cannot make it back existed without any type of incident or accident, as if there had been nothing there in the first place. Above the darkened planet, the coffins of the cosmos festered brilliantly. Behold! Death showed itself again. People consumed doses of fantasy[5] and adjusted death's margin of error. So many lives were created and then erased. Walking standing disappearing appearing, death repeated itself erratically. No one could predict when death would draw close. Life carried on. Every morning wives poured cereal into plates and husbands spread newspapers on the kitchen table and children spilled cereal submerged in milk on the newspapers. All of them silently left the table and cleaned up and swallowed their fantasy and left for the day and returned to reality in the evening. The wives set out white plates and the husbands cut up pieces of roast duck and the fat on the children's plates hardened. Everyone hastened to face reality, then they cleaned up and went into their rooms and swallowed their fantasies and went to bed. Intercourse[6] and masturbation[7] followed. I want to rest now. The fantasies of those who face death were always the same. People secretly looked forward to death. After everyone went to sleep. It was about time to conquer the cosmos and death began worrying about living absent-mindedly. Why do people pretend so naturally like they're living? Now revealed for the first time, Steven Paul Smith (1969–2003) began writing about death.[8]

NOTES

1) Death was once 1 kilometer in diameter. Every year it grew little by little; it has now reached 10 kilometers. If it crashes into Earth, it would have an estimated force of 3.85 million megatons.

2) A kind of cover-type bomb action figure that hangs by both ends on a designated airship for explosives and designed to wrap the bottom half of death.

3) They were modeled after the New Right, the explosives team affiliated with the death planet.

4) A small cosmos tube by Kitchen Knives Corp, designed to deal with immature death.

5) New Moon antidepressants called Roman Candle, XO, etc. Effective against unusual sadness, anxiety, and accompanying symptoms of depression. Physical changes due to toxicity may occur with long-term use or abuse. In fact, the woman who used this fantasy for long-term became 2:45 a.m.

6) Here, the usage of the term is restricted to the act of heterosexual couple Gray and Bunny Smith who, for the purposes of reproduction by means of sperm uniting with egg, inserted penis into vagina and, through mutual friction, resulted in instinctive ejaculation.

7) The act of using hand, foot or other item to stimulate one's genitals in order to feel the pleasure of intercourse as well as to care for one's own

feelings. In Omaha, Nebraska, depending on the color of consolation, they are sorted into the white of the eye and the iris.

8) I'm so sorry—love Elliott, God forgive me. 10.21.2003.

Dylan[1)]

Dylan was planted at Saint Vincent Botanical Garden[2)] three years ago. The following is a film about her.

It was a Friday night, unlike other Friday nights, when the deep green of the ivy cracked open the window. Dylan shut the copy of *Blowin' in the Wind* that she was reading and stood in front of the full-length mirror. She lowered her pants and removed her panties. She spread open her legs and bent from her waist. With both of her hands, slowly, she parted her buttocks. She could see the tender buds sprouting from the round of her anus. Dylan opened and closed and opened and closed her buttocks. It was instinctual.

It had been several months past one hundred years since Dylan had left for Minnesota. In Dylan's time, her skin sagged and drooped blue and blue. Wide, green moss covered the soiled testicles and penis. Tidy straight hair turned into disheveled purple hair. The vitality of death overflowed with life.

A letter flew in from Dylan. Every day, Dylan held the letter and headed into the night. She basked in the clouds and swayed in the direction the moon blows. As he turned into a fresh skeleton, Dylan was soaked to the bone with an unforgettable sense of satisfaction.

Dylan opened the envelope. Her toenails fell off and her toes that had been torn up to her ankles writhed. Dylan admired the lively roots. Thinking that the transformation is agreeable to the essence of plants, she sent a prayer of thanks to her mother in heaven. She held up the telephone receiver. Put it back down. She set fire to Dylan's letter.

Zimmerman, caretaker of vegetative humans,[3] carefully moved Dylan to a coffin. In the rattling dark on the way to Saint Vincent Botanical Garden, Dylan's eyeballs gave off the smell of dead tears and fell out. The eye sockets closed and were wiped out. Two pointed ears fell off and disappeared without a sound. The low nose sank even lower.

Dylan, planted at Rotolo Flower Garden, was the perfect plant specimen. Her fan-shaped violet petals and her long, thin green stem were natural. Only then did Dylan's human lips, wondering how many years a mountain can exist before it is washed to sea, spit Dylan out and shut themselves tight. That was the end and the beginning of her being named Dylan.

Dylan was classified as a silentshadeplant.

NOTES

1) According to *Blowin' in the Wind*, Saint Vincent Botanical Garden's encyclopedia of plants, Dylan is a female plant that grows in the relatively low light and damp conditions of the botanical garden. In bright light, on the other hand, the growth of the plant is hampered and results in its death. It bears one flower exactly once during the winter solstice. The white pollen that disperses once the bud opens is referred to as "breath."

2) A botanical garden located in Minnesota, which gets its name from the hospital in which Dylan Thomas breathed his last. Caretaker Robert Allen

Zimmerman has been responsible for managing the garden from end to beginning.

3) A term used to refer to people who think physical sex (animalness) and mental gender (vegetativeness) are the opposite. It was originally used to allude to patients who were addicted to chlorophyll.

What Do Angels Do on Silent and Holy Nights;
Duane and Michals took a sequence of photos of
angels returning home after attending a party and
edited them into one photo. The following is an exhibit
featuring an angel who escaped from the photo.
Therefore, a posture of proper appreciation is required.

Marilyn Monroe opens the door and steps into the darkness. They hover in the light. She takes off her halter dress. Her pearl-gray underwear is dull. With her neck now light, she steps out of her red heels and vanishes like fog. They hover in the light. She gradually reappears. Once she's reappeared, she grabs a bottle of time and pours it down her throat. She presses close her wide and bright lips and smiles. She is holding the bottle by its long neck. Everything is fleeting and she is standing still like her empty bottle. She is erased one by one. They hover in the light. She picks up the telephone receiver and, letting the cord hang, crumbles away. She places time on a square book. She does not unfold her words. She is reading to herself. She is being demolished. Cradling the telephone to her chest, she hovers in the light. They, who were hovering in the light, become stained behind the blue bottle. By the window, even her lipstick is erased. Only her beauty mark remains. She opens the window like it is her destiny. They, who can now be seen, hover in the light. There are breasts and a grave on her naked body. She puts both hands neatly behind her neck. Her sparse pubic hair is visible. The hanging mound of her genitals is barely invisible. She lowers her head. Two girls with Rudolph's red noses hanging from their faces, following behind them and the piercingly bright crippled man

opens night. She throws out the phone. The phone stops for a moment between floor 15.5 and floor 15.[2] From the small round holes of the telephone receiver, black snow pours out and whispers. ❀❀ ❀❀❀ ❀ ❀❀. The voice falls and shatters. She is the only one growing darker alone. Looking into her two eyes, I take my eyes off the telescope. Far off, a small bird[3] taps at the window. The voices of the girls singing carols were like shiny noses that, had I seen them, I would have thought were on fire. I hear the girls' song like misfired firecrackers. I . . . hold the wings in front of the telescope again. At the blatantly open window, her somber gold wig does not fly. Behind it, next to her knocked-over high heels, in front of her wrinkled dress, under the shattered time, a stained copy of darkness lies on top of a heap of feathers. In the world outside the telescope, a blizzard is fluttering for the first time in seven years.[4] Soft, white souls fly toward and stick to the glass window. Carrying the white light on its head, crippling death crosses the street with a gigantic sickle. He is following two guides and heading to this place. They hover in the dark light. Like the hands of a clock, they see me and her at the same time.

NOTES

1) August 5, 1962. You are correct if you recall an actual incident that occurred on that date, near Joe DiMaggio's house. Following two girls and one crippled man, a woman disappeared into the outskirts of night. Because of how surprisingly fictional the incident seemed, the readers from the area, including myself, were greatly shocked. I believe this should remain an unsolved mystery.

2) August 5, 1962. That year photographer Joe DiMaggio catches on film the falling to death of one woman, which he will witness one night of that year. This staged photo, which captures one moment of a woman jumping off a high-rise building cradling a telephone to her chest, is on display at The Asphalt Jungle film archives on floor 15.

3) August 5, 1962. The film White Bird included in Norma Jeane Mortenson, released by Joe DiMaggio's record label, refers to the following facial expression: "The winterbilledwhitebird sings, when the tiny woman dies in the color black, no one will remember her girlhood. Not even she herself."

4) August 5, 1962. To honor the death of Marilyn Monroe, Joe DiMaggio's drag queens held a show by the following name in a copy of a book: *They Remember Her Dress That Stood in Dry Ice Every Night after Going Out for the First Time in Seven Years.*

Tale of the Qishi Girl (漆室女傳)[1]

It is told, the view of love (戀愛觀) of the Qishi girl, from the town of Qishi in the state of Nao (猱), is going big or going home. She knows the joy of growing unripe peppers and the joy of picking ripe peppers, so she goes around seducing the hottest fellas. And her flirting technique is quite peculiar (奇奇).

So even if the Qishi girl sets her heart on starting a romantic relationship and goes round and round and round and round Chang'an (長安) a–gain with her white, bursting thighs exposed through a blue (靑) skirt, hardly any fellas come onto her. So she sits cross-legged on a slat bench and blows a bugle and sings a song of offering wine (勸酒歌)[2] under the moonlit night (月三更).

The ingenious melody is so sorrowful yet sensual that it even vanquishes Duke Zhou of Ding's daughter Qing He (淸河)'s[3] technique for absorbing men's vigor (吸精導氣法).[4] And she dizzyingly seduces the joyful (樂) gang of drunken boys (酊少年)[5] who are effortlessly walking the path of the will-o'-the-wisp (燐道) over the wall of barrels (壜).

Older boys sit in a row on the wall of a willow tree tale (談), and, bumping the front of the rubber canvas shoes, they pluck the string (弦) of Danga Danga and say huzzah. They volunteer to backbite about Nanjang (亂場) the Qishi girl, who sweet-talks even to the moonlight.

They say, "bingo," and look at it, and it is your leg.

They say, "that's right," and look at it, and it is your middle leg.

The Qishi girl does not let go the bird of climax (絶頂) and falls down as she sneakily clings on to pink shoes on the walls (堵牆) and chirps. A drunken boy who's at a loss jumps over the wall and erects her stiffly in his arms. Youth.

Unripe pepper spectators are also cocked, hard and red; all types of cockling holes appear in the sky's paper door (門風紙); the moon grandma too hurriedly cocks a jaundiced eye; at length, from the Qishi girl's flirting technique, a sentence (文章) cocks itself tensely.

The fellas the Qishi girl flirted like this would fit into 108 carts. The Qishi girl's flirting technique, called the "Collection and Battle Technique of the Qishi Girl" (漆室女採戰之術), is circulated in the party halls across the state of Lu (盧),[6] but who cares. Today, again, our Qishi girl is merely dum de dum de dicking around without any thoughts (無念無想) in order to softly erect her unique technique for being an exemplary woman.

NOTES

1) Included in *Oral Biographies of Exemplary Women*, written by Ru Fang (乳房) several days before the state of Song (慅) melted down. Depending on the edition, they are called the "Biography of Cho from Gye-dong," "Biography of Heo from Sinnae," etc. The original copy is kept in the sand drift (流砂) of the Ice Village and is wandering around every nook and cranny of the country.

2) A song people sing as they offer wine while adding a footnote (註釋) at a drinking party (酒席).

3) A woman who was honored to be a teacher of Xia Ji (夏姬), the daughter of a carpenter from the state of Zheng (鄭). She is known to have become intimate with men while becoming younger three times after getting old, becoming a queen three times, becoming a wife seven times, and becoming a widow nine times.

4) A technique for absorbing a man's sexual vigor and drawing in his material energy. By making a man feel ecstatic during sex, a woman takes away the man's *yang* energy and repletes her *yin* energy. It is widely known to have the quickest and surest effect among all the techniques for overcoming physical ageing and restoring youth.

5) This refers to drunken Bohemians who loiter in packs, without an interest in improving themselves through study or moral cultivation.

6) It appears that the name of the state was confused while the text is being engraved (板刻), but I transcribe as it is.

Ashes of Time

As Ouyang Feng walked the desert where once had been an ocean, he thought,[1] *If I went back in time, I'd be able to stroll along the beach, thick with peach blossoms, and see the season's first snowfall with Leslie Cheung. But isn't that impossible for me?*[2] Ouyang Feng stopped walking and dug a hole in the sand. He buried a piece of white bone from his neck. A puddle formed. He wet his throat. The puddle dried up. How many more collarbones would he need to leave this planet of sand? Ouyang Feng moved his body, which was slowly becoming boneless. The sun pursued him doggedly.[3] Ouyang Feng sagged little by little to the ground. *Tomorrow, I will reform into tomorrow's skeleton.* Ouyang Feng stared into the hole in the sand where the pale pink saltwater should have been sloshing around.[4] Softly, a single petal of a peach blossom appeared like a mirage and then vanished without a trace. *Would that I could nullify the time slipping away from us.*[5] Ashes of time in the sky grew apart and the night rolled in. Ouyang Feng pulled the bamboo hat over his eyes and thought of time. *Everything is my fault.* Ouyang Feng pulled a red pouch from the depths of his chest. He opened the pouch. It was an ankle bone from time that he had received from Leslie Cheung. He put his lips to the bone and smelled a light floral fragrance.[6] Everything turned back into the oceans of time. Ouyang Feng faultlessly collapsed into the sand hole, where the darkness was flailing.

His skin turned red and ripe until the sun set and the moon rose. It turned blue and cooled off.[7] Ouyang Feng's moist pupils looked like tidepools that had just formed. His eyes soon vanished. The sandstorm that carries his bones began to form Ouyang Feng's ankle bones.[8]

NOTES

1) Back in the day, I used to look at the mountain and wonder what was over it.

2) I don't know why I did that. I couldn't help myself. When I left, I felt his tears on my face, drying.

3) The first day of spring had passed. It is now the day on which insects wake. Friends usually came to see me around this time, but this year they did not.

4) I thought I had won. But one day, I looked into the mirror and realized I had lost. Because when I was at my most beautiful, the one I loved was not by my side.

5) They say the reason humans suffer so much is because of memory. That year onward, I forgot many things and only remembered that I loved peach blossoms.

6) The only thing I can do for something I do not have is not forgetting it.

7) If a sword cuts fast enough, the sound of gushing blood sounds pleasant, like a breeze . . . I never thought I would hear that sound coming from my own blood.

8) The flag does not move, the breeze does not move either. Only your heart moves.

say it
when the last night falls gently upon you

you have a story to tell and
you can topple it like snow or erect it like a monument

that night when all was orderly
when the fog came roiling upon you
hear it
the very first prayer you held

your horror
your hollowness
your lie

sing it, little by little
your concrete world is melting and
you come to exist so that we cannot touch you, but,
faith or belief does not exist or is extinguishing,
how accurately it captures the mystery of death

the first light spills upon you like black ink
when you were lying down, alive, for a moment

One   second later
Thirty   hours later
Three hundred sixty days later

the memories that will be useless anyway,
always remember them

drunkards loitering until morning
demonstration of a peaceful reading
oral sex on each other at night

that's right, S
last night we said all that we needed to say
like a gaggle of geese

be silent*

NOTES

* I wish for my closing remarks to be a eulogy for your death. Now or then
  there will be fewer things to add and more things to take out in my speech,
  and I'll look upon that time with a serenity, like a lap blanket. So now,

* Now, my opening remark is not a commentary on your life. Now or then,
  your two pupils float like water droplets, and when I raise my two palms,
  spread open by your death, I will remember this quiet humanity for your
  sake.

An Illustration of Time by the Merry Pranksters*

The Merry Pranksters, who will throw themselves into the future, clamor for a taste of time. The Merry Pranksters open the right ventricle of the past and, in the season of fog and rain, close the window. The Merry Pranksters open the left ventricle of the past and, in the season of snow and wind, close the window. Tonight, a sunbeam in the shape of a flock of pigeons will enter the closed hearts of the Merry Pranksters.

The Merry Pranksters imagined the Merry Pranksters wandering through time.

The Merry Pranksters read geisha coffee. The Merry Pranksters drink Newtonian physics for ladies. The Merry Pranksters crack their joints for a dance. The Merry Pranksters become useless with every step.

The Merry Pranksters came under the influence of time wandering through The Merry Pranksters.

The geisha's paper umbrella is red, wet, with daring. The geisha cuts through the rain and walks toward the snow-covered field. Her white hair crumbles away because of that. The old geisha, abandoned by whomever, lies down at the end of the world. In the bright midnight snowfield, a red spider blooms with determination.

The Merry Pranksters drank time, adjusting the transparent label of its can.

The Merry Pranksters's black hair turns white in barely a second. It is a white night. The Merry Pranksters, Merry Pranksters, Merry Pranksters, one by one, convene by the window. The Merry Pranksters open their right eye. A misty rain blows through half of the sunshine. The gay Sha laughs and cries. The eye closes. The Merry Pranksters open their left eye. A blizzard gusts through half of the sunshine. The abandoned gay Sha cries and laughs. The eye closes. The Merry Pranksters are already blinded by the one red spider disappearing through the middle of sunshine. From within time, I reject becoming clear.*

The Merry Pranksters put down the label, not yet dry and nowhere to be found, and open the window. They take off lightly amid the weathers. The Merry Pranksters take a tub of hallucination, the Merry Pranksters take a shot of reading, the Merry Pranksters take a volume of dancing all at once. The Merry Pranksters return to tomorrow night and sit down at their desk and begin to draw with open eyes.

The Merry Pranksters devoted their lives to dying through the manufacture* of time.

NOTES

* American author Ken Kesey lived separately but together with a group of people in a house in the state of the Beatles. These people rejected clarity, calling indistinctly for the use of the hallucinatory drug, time.

* Operation code made right before the Merry Pranksters offed themselves; they sketched time with clarity until their death. It is better known as lyrics to the song "Beatles" by Sgt. Pepper's Miss Lonelyhearts Club Band.

* Referring to the label attached to time that is hiding unclear efficacy. They drew plenty of only drawing of the red spider, obtained through the collapse of the world. One of these drawings was also used as the cover for the Beatles's thirteenth full-length album released in 1971, *Time*.

Those days[1]

Henry was the kind of person who often got his feelings hurt when people called him a sissy boy. Not only Henry James, but also Henry and James, who became a hairy plumber and balding naval officer after they grew up, were the kind of people who held a hammer and nail. Around the time they were a plumber and a naval officer, the word "homo" spread throughout the public toilets. In the face of that era, Henry focused on the Henry and Laura who appeared in "Nail and Hammer."

Those days

Laura asked Henry to go on a quiet date. Laura felt inexpressibly allured by taciturn Henry who was fascinated with novels like *Henry's Youth with Rugby and Cheerleaders*. Laura agreed with Henry, *Of course, ABBA is the best.*

Those days

Henry grew up. Every wedding anniversary, without fail, Henry gave Henry a Henry Records ABBA LP as a gift. The last time Henry came by with an LP for Henry, Henry, who was reading James Henry's "Anniversary," tapped Henry's buttocks. Henry went up to his room. Henry shouted. Henry had nothing to say. Henry fell asleep.

Those days

James Henry finished writing *Laura Came Back*. Henry needed to leave Laura. Henry needed to stay with Laura. Henry and Laura faithfully divided up the roles of loser and winner according to personality and taste. *The winner takes it all, of course.* Every night, instead of Laura, Henry listened to the song that Henry left behind and that Laura couldn't throw away.

Those days

Henry, who bid farewell to the sick Henry, pulled back the curtain of death in the small apartment situated on the stage of love. The death that had been prepared was clean. A desire for life no longer plagued Henry's final performance, so brilliant sunlight had been hung for those who had died alone instead of dark rain clouds. It was like the weather at the funeral of a writer who would always be known as *Cliché*.

Those days

Laura had begun living with Henry, and she bade farewell to Henry without attending his funeral. Following the rhetorical expression of Laura, in the middle of the night, Laura read James Henry's *Henry Dies*. At their regular Saturday evening dinner parties, Laura played an irrelevant dinner plate instead of the Henry Records LP.

Those days

Henry had oral sex with Henry. Henry was the son of Mrs. Laura who had attended Henry's funeral. Before that, Henry decided to delight Henry by dancing to ABBA songs. Henry said it first, *One day, just one time, I saw Henry's soul dancing to ABBA*. Henry was an ~~adorable man. In *Pink Hair, Pink Lipstick*, James Henry commem~~orated Henry's passing as such:

And thus, in those days,
In the end, we will all be winners

Those Days

Laura and Henry became a long-standing couple of the Chiquitita family. Henry and Henry left for Greenwich Village. And O! Henry opened a show to "Dancing Queen" and became a heavenly drag queen. That was how James Henry ended those days.[2]

NOTES

1) A book that was written with nothing written in it, and the writer who hadn't written anything flipped open.

2) James Henry was a writer who hadn't written anything. His non-works include: Book *That Was Written with Nothing Written in It and the Writer Who Hadn't Written Anything, Henry's Youth with Cheerleaders and Rugby, Cliché, Henry Came Back, Laura Dies, Pink Hair and Gold Lipstick*, and *Write the Novel, the Novel; Those Days*.

1

Blackbird Hector steps into Room 584 of an old Los Angeles motel.[2] *Goddammit*, Hector removes the dark-blue two-button suit spread thickly with blood and safely gets into bed. He pulls at the light switch and a scarlet heat appears. This place is not a part of the city. In a voice tinged with darkness, Hector pulls at the chill of the comforter and covers himself. The

    LA Angel

appears.

> Fallen in the snow,
> the benevolent pupils of the nightbird
> is filled with the face of child, eyes closed
> O so fleeting nightbird, softly fluttering nightbird
> You sing of dying life even as you lie there dead

Sleep well. Who buried her in the dirt, the Mother who sang lullabies in a broken voice? Blackbird Hector turns his face into the black alleyways of his pillow.

2

James Franco started to repeat the nameless Mother's lullaby. James Franco was high as a kite[3] when the nameless Mother gave birth to him all by herself underneath the tree of life. James Franco, holding his breath between the nameless Mother's legs, *Kiddo, don't forget* ~~*what I first ...... of this world.*~~ James Franco remembered the dying Mother's voice. For the first time, James Franco folded a corner. To James Franco, the dead, nameless Mother was a classic.

3

The night slowly passed over the stump of the moon.
Go back
to before you were born
to the quiet, lifeless nest

Blackbird Hector is politely growing cold. High on drugs, James Franco was beyond sleep. Hector pulls off the stiff comforter and looks inside the deep hole.[4] James Franco saw the beak of darkness slowly opening wider and wider. The sheets are vast and stained darkly red. James Franco smoothed down a mysterious engraved spot on the bed carved by naked lovers. The place where the L O V E night was the very first to fly down and build a nest, and the very last to lay eggs. Our dead Mother might still be alive over there. Hector turns his exhausted body to a full-length mirror hanging on the right-hand wall. James Franco gazed at the desolate man in the mirror. A huge flying object burst through the two pupils inside of the two hours that could not look at each other. Hector opened his mouth, and James Franco soundlessly recited poetry.

Hector, you idiot
Why were you in our territory?
We were just petty thieves
You stole small things so grandly
That's right, you only stole peoples' hearts

4

A beautiful, weary woman who died without a name flies down next to them and lies down. She embraces them and lets out a warbling lullaby. She remembers. The night they held the leaves of the tree of life in their mouths and flew down between her legs. Room 584 of an old Los Angeles motel is dying. He covers his glory hole with his chest.[5] Petty bastard, why didn't you stay in your territory? In your safe space, where you've stolen everyone's hearts. In your mother's breast. From within that breast, he pulls the light switch. At last, the nightbird flies off into the night. The

LA Angel

appears.

Come here, child
Look at the stars shining through your window
Look at the dawn breaking over the welfare Center for the Blind
Look at the sunlight streaming through the holes in your corpse

5

On a winter night long past, a bird that had been shot with a gun was discovered in a Los Angeles motel. The spot that fell like a feather in the city district where the film *First of the Gang to Die* is being screened in a double feature.[6]

NOTES

1) From now on, all the songs that will be featured here will be sung by dead voices, not deafened voices.—To Morrissey

2) When James Franco, who had spent most of his youth as a day laborer, discovered ragged Gifford's *First of the Gang to Die* in motel room 584, the still young James Franco dreamed of a dead gang for the first time.

3) After leaving the forest, James Franco now stands on the beach and watches a single, giant tree rise out of the ocean. The tree looks like a bird sitting on the water. When the leaves flap, time crashes against the shore. Every time this happens, James watches Hector, who was born from a dead body. To James Franco, Hector looks like a young James Franco and an old Hector. The dead Mother flies to and fro. James Franco plunges into the water and walks toward the tree, the bird, and the Mother.

4) Hector followed the UFO and stepped into the nighttime bathroom tucked between the stars. James, Hector borrowed water and fire from the aliens. Hector lit up the fire on water. The alien, fiddling with the UFO after making an emergency landing, asked, *Will I be able to get back through the black hole safely? I have to live.*

5) Face drenched, James Franco gazed at the glory hole around which angel wings were drawn. A glory hole shaped like a punctured UFO moved little by little to the smoke of Hector's cigarette. At the same time, the two of them pressed their pupils to their glory holes. The giant tree that had given birth to the forest above the bird-covered beach was now carrying a new life.

6) About the actor's birth: "He said he started singing with the lyrics that were published in the *New York Times*. And the time, I was there, in his district, paving the road in the winter, during the nights in Los Angeles.

So I was very confident, with a dead voice, I would be able to inhabit Hector." James Franco, *Glamor*. See January 11 interview.

o) Dedicated to Terrence Mallick, with much respect and gratitude

The Last Blotch

Coal dust flew The blotch was familiar with night surging through the world of broken windows A powdery night nowhere to be found by no one at all The blotch shook its stiff, negligee-wings Yellow meridians embroidered on the wings patterned time The night particles gently dispersed, thickened The sound of wings soundlessly circling the insignificant, crash-landed remnants of humanity Within a great muteness the blotch held erect its one thousand Technicolor antennae Over pieces of broken glass the blotch once again plays the memories that will darken from the middle

Before light disappeared from our world

The Island [1)]
travelled between this place and the bright white light,
transporting upright beasts covered in their sleep

Before coal disappeared from our world

There was a coal miner on that island
He was machinery
He was a facsimile
He was the last person to remember his lover

Before love disappeared from our world

He was half dead from love
He alone was a parasite among humans
He used his memory as collateral
He became blotched through the blotches

Before our world disappeared

The blotch lowered its antennae The future of the past still could not be revealed Therefore death was already meaningful to the blotch The blotch pulled back the yellow meridians On the roof of the Saemaeul train[2] the dark melancholy fell in sheets The blotch closed its dreary eyes The glass pieces turned black The crustacean's shadow sank to the floor of the night With eyes closed, the blotch stared at the skeleton and the rusted machinery that had lost light and coal and love Water seeped into the things that had lost their usefulness In the far future our love cannot be excavated Into one coal miner's heart, the blotchy water[3] fell with a plip plop And the remaining time passed little by little by little

Before light disappears from our world . . . before coal disappears from the world . . . before love disappears from our world . . . before our world disappears . . .

NOTES

1) The longest coal-mine train in the universe and a triumph of human technology. The train was named after the very first island mine.

2) Although originally for coal transport, with the launch of the Galaxy Express Migration Company, all trains changed their names and their routes from left to right, leading to the forced deportation of past-expired human clones, robots marked for disposal whose spare parts are no longer manufactured, and no-longer-useful humans.

3) Fond of lonely, humid, human-like places, it usually lives within useless human things. Although it is carnivorous and eats memories, it lives symbiotically with microbiota in its intestine, and they decompose and absorb the solitary fibers (cellulose 5) of memory. Usually found widespread on Planet 3, but due to the planetary migration policy, its habitat has moved to Planets 6, 9, 15, and the like.

Polonaise
—à la Mishima and Yukio

It had been a week since the old security guard went missing. Yukio looked out through the angular golden glow of the window. Little by little, the leaves of the trees lining the flower bed had become tinged with a clear, blood-red color. Yukio fiddled with a sheathed dagger and hummed a polonaise.[1]

*

The sound of the grandfather clock striking twelve rang through the long, dark hallway. Mishima, who was stretched out on top of his desk in front of the podium, sat up stiffly. Mishima's pale white face stood out even in the darkness. His make-up was neat like a kabuki actor's. With eyes half-dead, Mishima rummaged through the desk drawer. He applied polonaise[2]-colored lipstick and weakly moved his stained lips.

Moonlight gushed abundantly into the silent classroom. The shadows of the polonaise[3]-adorned trees swelled. Mishima stood up and, for no reason, began twirling his body and bobbing his head. He ran his hands slowly down his chest and stretched them straight into the air and left them there. His bony wrists trembled and snapped. The owl wearing the Mask of Confessions cried out and Mishima uselessly danced to it.

Creak creak creak creak. Someone was walking down the hallway to a beat. Mishima kept a smile on his face, as if his mouth had been ripped apart, and stopped dancing. Mishima floated to the classroom door within an *eek eek.* The footsteps slowly grew closer. *Creak.* Through the glass window of the door, Mishima came face to face with Yukio. Like girls, they sweetly brought their lips together. As time went by smoothly, Mishima returned to his desk and put his head down. He removed a piece of his shattered neck and carved into the name that was carved in the corner. Yukio stood there for a while and gazed at shattered Mishima from behind. *Who's there?*

The security guard shone his flashlight in Yukio's direction. Yukio turned his inexpressible face from the light. He closed his eyes and walked, step by step. *I meet myself in the classroom every night,* he sang. The old security guard took a slow step backward. The polonaise[4] melody filled the hallway, and through the window, glimmered the dark pupils of the trees. Yukio wiped his eyes with his sleeve. A few strands of teardrops that had fallen onto his shoulder muscles fell to the ground. The security guard finally lost his light. The two of them darted off into the thick darkness of the hallway.

*

Nameless chrysanthemum petals fell on top of the inverted Yukio Mishima's name. It was the seventeenth spring that snow had fallen. At the back of the classroom, Yukio, his face buried in the desk, plucked pears without anyone knowing. Mishima, whose fair, dead face fluttered. Mishima Yukio heard the sound of waves.

NOTES

1) Since it vanished without a trace, it is no surprise that no one else remembers Mishima and Yukio's polonaise. Even on the cassette tape they once gave me, only the songs that took the lead and fell behind the time exist. Still, whenever I hear or read the lyrics of "Meet Me in the Classroom at Night," which they scrawled for me on a piece of pink paper, I exhaust myself trying to suppress the urge to run to the classroom in the middle of the night and dance. Apropos of nothing, if you'd like to listen to the polonaise song, I can lend you the tape.

2) An ornamental tree we grew since the time we were each other's first loves. Because of its unique red leaves, it is known as Blood Feeder or Thirst for Love.

3) The most representative style of clothing during the Black Lizard period. The overskirts were inflated by several layers of glamor and romance, which made up both sides of the outfit as well as the bum, creating a kind of cylindrical instability. They were usually worn by tottering young ladies.

4) Dance music for "a sadness, gradually slowing down." Around the time the School of Flesh's seminar on depravity withered in overall popularity, the seminar became trendy among the patriotic youth.

You, old girl.

Girl who escaped the room[6] where the deep, wide dream flows.

You, drooping girl.

Girl with gray hair hanging to ankles thin and blue.

Girl searching for the always-lovely daughter of the daughter who looked just like always-lovely Nanny.

Nanny, Nanny, please comb my hair.

Girl who will steal Nanny's dreams before she dies.

Girl who rubs static electricity with whale skin.

Girl unfolding the translucent face that Nanny brought.

Whale! Whale! Whale!

Wailing wailing wailing girl.

Nanny, this face isn't lovable at all.

Suffocating girl with a shiitake-colored face.

In the dim light, Raju Handique looked into the face of the old girl peeping into his dream. *No matter how you look at it, it is an unlovable face.* Raju Handique got ready to leave. The moonlight knot came undone. The darkness had creased eyelids. The mystery of the old girl gathered in corners of Raju Handique's eyes. Raju Handique looked again at the old girl's starlight. You lost your face. Raju Handique moved his thin legs in the old girl's direction. Moment that had passed in a moment. The old girl poked Raju Handique's eye and squirmed. Bug! Bug! Bug! Raju Handique's face was torn to shreds. Raju Handique escaped to the white forest[7] where the old girl's soul dwells.

✳

That night, two crescent moons in the shape of eyebrows came together in a frown.

Surprised, the oldest girl of the village half closed her eyes.

Miss! Miss! Our old Miss!

When would she close her eyes?

The always-lovely daughter of the daughter who looked like always-lovely Nanny sang a song.

The hair that had grown oink oink oinking long came flying to the young lady. She sang.

Decisive mold grew in the young lady's face. She completely died while singing.

The young lady's gray hair turned into a flood of water.

Winter came first with three feet, then with two feet, then finally with four feet.

The young lady lost herself. Around the time her dream disappeared, two spiders in the forest floated back in time. The lady was known as Miss Dreaming Human-Faced Spider.[8]

✳

Raju Handique, who had lost his face, cut the thread hanging from his butthole and had an eye on whether this was a dream, or a carpet, or a story. Water droplet, barely visible to the eye. Raju Handique decided never to dream of a person's face again. Spider! Spider! Spider! The face of the mysterious girl who had brushed Raju Handique's fate once long ago flickered and then vanished. Raju Handique erased the human face left with him. Dawn was breaking. Finally, the cosmos had begun.[9]

NOTES

6) A type of idiom used in place of "sound sleep" (a very deep and restful slumber, an uninterrupted sleep). It is often used in the southwest region of life.

7) A hidden word used in the asshole of the southwest region of life. Refers to the ghost forest, the young lady's snow-white pubic hair, and the girl's gray hair. The meaning changes from person to person.

8) Song sung by spiderfaces living in the bathroom alley of the southwest region of life, so they can sleep soundly. "The young lady whose eyes are now forever closed, the young lady who is now gone forever, the young human-faced spider lady who is now gone and dreaming"—these lyrics were repeated in different pitches.

9) Raju Handique, who lived in a cobweb in the southwest region of life, sat on the toilet as day was breaking and spread open the asshole One Thousand and One Arabian Nights that Raju Handique had passed on by spinning the web behind the back of the Upanishads. Life had begun.

The base was built. All thanks to the power of man, unstoppable by the power of man. With that, the moon disappeared. The waves sank. From the depths of the ocean, where the circulating blue midnight had disappeared, the alveoli of those who held their breaths bubbled to the surface. Like ejaculate of the dead moon. In the future, no one would live in the base ever again. The base is merely empty. Nameless battleships offered their condolences and disappeared. The base's uncut nucleus shed its outer skin. It grew. It stood erect. Took aim, fired. Sometimes clearly identifiable, transnational ghost ships couldn't slip past the base and were destroyed. Pascal, the faces need to move back. The faces need to move back and be people hiding in the village of the base. While Pascal was silent, the faces tried searching for the exhaustion of a human turning into a human again, from far off, where lungs were swollen with water. The base widened on its own. Avoiding the base's piston motion, the faces faced extinction. The mitochondria of the extinct lowered onto the shoulders of the living creatures. Red eyes. The faces pressed the shoulders together, drooping by one Hertz each, and piled up their breaths on one another. Pascal tried to cut across time. The faces all talked about the failed maneuver. *Pascal, the faces have only one chance left.* The base was devastated magnificently. The faces gathered at the center of the base. The faces fused together and exploded. White and black. A hole appeared in the ocean. The base widens the base to the base to the base to the base. The base quickly and precisely expands toward the island. Having passed the hole, Pascal embraced cutting-edge anxiety and arrived at the entrance of the hard, rocky beach. Red-footed-horse-crap crabs violently caught moonlight alive in their pincers and moved in a line to the left, to the left. Pascal moved the dp5 toward the future base at the end of the beach. Pascal's footsteps in the past slowly grew more and more defined.#

NOTES

William Basinski's music. Pascal grows clearer as the day breaks. Heading to the village of the base, we come across Future Pascal. That's when a translucent face appears on the screen. That's when a translucent face also appears on the screen. That's when even a translucent face appears on the screen. The music will now flow out for 25 minutes and 11 seconds. We watch but see nothing. The music stops. The beach's final chapter.

William Basinski's music. Pascal fades out as the day breaks. Heading to the base, we move with Future Pascal. That's when your face emerges on-screen. That's when your face also makes its debut on-screen. That's when even your face makes its debut on-screen. The music will now flow in for 25 minutes and 11 seconds. We do but do nothing. The music stops. The beach's final chapter explosion.

Regarding Cate Blanchett's Dream[1)]

At an outdoor cafe in Geneva, I discovered a photograph. Of the gazes that looked at the actress's dream from various angles, one was an image called Cate Blanchett.

Cate Blanchett found a vanishing point in the dream of the Cate Blanchett published in *Esquire*. It was a single, innumerably small vanishing point emerging from her own face, which she had seen countless times yet had never seen before.

I closed my eyes and recorded a dot on Cate Blanchett's face. Cate Blanchett's dotted face was reflected on the lens of the dark room again. I started filming. Who stuck Cate Blanchett's face on the dot?

Cate Blanchett said one recently excavated drop of vanishing point looked like a letter from the soon-vanished country of Lu and drew back. A blurry letter from the past carrying the meaning of long ago, blind, human, with tearful eyes. Even today Cate Blanchett realized that she had wandered through time.

One month, Borges with his eyes shut learned how to read through touch. Brushing away the dust marring the gold leaf, he listened to the titles and gave his ear to the sounds of the bookcase falling toward silence. Up until he expanded his never-ending dream in Geneva, Borges used his soul to read the music of the universe.[2]

Soon, I am coming across the soul of Borges, whose eyes are open because he is blind. There developed a tremor below his right eye. The wide-eyed blind ignoramus's world extended even to Cate Blanchett. Borges hung up long-ago Cate Blanchett; blind Cate Blanchett; human Cate Blanchett; Cate Blanchet with tearful eyes to dangle like fruit.[3]

I shot a film at a place in Geneva where there was no one else. I stuck on eyelashes. I picked up a foreign novel instead of the script. I am at the filming location and then I disappeared. I received a text message. *I put a dot on your face*, I muttered to myself. One by one, mouth closed, Cate Blanchett gathered water droplets that had slid down Cate Blanchett.[4]

I ordered a coffee. I handed over Cate Blanchett. I pulled out a cigarette. Cate Blanchett is at a place in Geneva where there is no one else. Cate Blanchett raises her eyelashes. Cate Blanchett opens up her foreign novel. Suddenly, Cate Blanchett becomes a non-existent entity at the filming location. Ghost, ghost, ghost. Cate Blanchett sends a text message. I found a vanishing point on my face, Cate Blanchett mutters to Cate Blanchett.[5]

Cate Blanchett looked at the Cate Blanchett published in *Esquire*. It was the Cate Blanchett who had been filming *I'm Not There* in Geneva. Cate Blanchett's dream came in at a glance. Cate Blanchett— who, long ago, had been a blind human with tearful eyes—saw a massive hand that was spraying a plant from which her dream hung like fruit. Borges sat down at a restaurant in Geneva and masturbated while stroking his soul's style.[6]

I met Cate Blanchett. My me is sitting at an outdoor cafe in Geneva and my me drinks coffee and my me smokes a cigarette and my me wonders if my me is me. Before Borges left a person for the dream, a piece of his soul vanished from *Esquire*. Regarding Cate Blanchett's dream, am I Cate Blanchett?[7]

I opened my eyes. I saw no one at all. I saw anything and everything. Sitting down at an outdoor cafe in Geneva, I put down my cup and stub out my cigarette and stroked the *Esquire*. The Cate Blanchett at the filming location wrapped herself up in the foreign novel and the coffee and the cigarette and in Cate Blanchett, and dreamed of fictional characters.[8]

The Cate Blanchett of the past opened her eyes once more. The filming location was not yet ready. Cate Blanchett left the golden-grass-colored *Esquire* on a chair and her eyes filled with tears. Looking for a mirror, Cate Blanchett escaped the filming location like a blind person. As though she had a dot or something she needed to check on right away.[9]

NOTES

1) Bach, Goldberg Variations, BWV 988, Aria. A movie and a novel and a poem start at the same time with Geneva as the setting. There is no conversation. Both voices could be heard at the same time.

2) Around 1886, in a Dresden library, Italian scholar of music Giamoto discovers a sketch of a musical composition. Presuming this will become

"Part of a Dream," the sonata composed by Borges around 1986, he completes "Adagio for Catherine" for string ensemble and two organs in G Minor, based on said sketch.

3) "Cate Blanchett begins while gazing at Cate Blanchett. While waiting for the soul of her father, who had passed away suddenly from a heart attack, eleven-year-old Cate Blanchett shoves the night away from her bed." See ~~Sarah Dahl's Photography Notes 1986–86.~~

4) Later, Todd Haynes will confess to sending Cate Blanchett the following text message, in order to be with her: "I've marked you in my heart since a long time ago. I've hoped you mark yourself with a dot and live as Jude."

5) In Jim Jarmusch's *Coffee and Cigarettes*, Cate Blanchett plays two characters, Cate and her cousin Shelly. At the hotel lounge where the promotional event takes place, Cate (Cate Blanchett) meets Shelly (Cate Blanchett), who looks just like her.

6) "The term 'style' originates from *stilus*, the name of a writing implement used in Ancient Rome. This refers not only to the shape of one's writing, but also encompasses the concept of composition, including the art of choosing the right word." Borges left behind a page of art history that he was fondling.

7) Cate Blanchett was born Catherine Blanchett. Cate Blanchett was cast as Katharine Hepburn in Martin Scorsese's *The Aviator*. In order to become Katherine, Cate dotted her whole body with freckles.

8) Cate Blanchett was unable to make the following people's dreams come true. Ridley Scott, Hannibal, Clarice Starling. Mike Nichols, Closer, Anna. Luis Buñuel, Regarding Cate Blanchett's Dream, Cate Blanchett.

9) "I remember being on the set of my first movie. The leading actor would read magazines or sleep whenever they had a spare moment. I thought (while acting on set), *how are they doing that?*" "If you know you're going to fail at something, fail gloriously!" Both voices could be heard at the same time. There is no conversation. A movie and a novel and a poem end at the same time with Geneva as the setting. Bach, Harpsichord Concerto No. 5 in F Minor, BWV 1056, Movement II: Largo.

Border[1]

✴

Once every one hundred years
in the borderlands of coincidence
where it is unclear if it will snow or not
when snow falls
the stain that appears at the bottom of the cup
after poppy tea is brewed and drunk
tells our fortune of a once-in-lifetime love[2]
The stain
flawlessly drawing a circle
giving off the color of a birch tree
refers to eternal love and death so sometimes
it holds captive the tenuous lovers in the room of tears
and locks the door

✴

It happened at Falls Border. Oscar[3] unfurled his wings and pulled
the trigger on Genet. Genet fell to the ground, pale lips agape. A
scarlet sentence of silence gushed forth from his heart. A white
feather read the light. *Lord, please allow me to go back to that time.*

Wiping off the fragments of rancid death splattered all over his face, Oscar inserted the barrel of the gun into his mouth. Long dark faced a deep dark. In an instant, Oscar, whose face and backside had vanished, whose front and back had overlapped, whose inside and outside had turned inside out, crashed into Genet's[4] wings. White light and divine grace descended from the heavens. The trumpet sounds of the angels who were to attach the two together in one, original body resounded. All the clocks in the world ran backwards. Following the route of migratory birds, the ankles of the white stars serenely crossed over the border.

❄

In the borderlands of Salon Reverie,[5] I am listening to a large parrot's song for wandering *slurpslurp*

Sipping flavorful poppy tea,

I tap on the keys of a typewriter as though it were your spine

Lovers have flocked to the border where snow falls to pledge their love

Trudging through the perilous canyon, the lovers scrubbed mysteriously at their skin and became sad and weary and no matter how much time passed without expression they saw no snow

When snow falls when snow falls

Atop the succulents at the border where the snow falls, the lovers' biting wish blew with a whoosh A wish met another wish and gave rise to suspicious flora

A huge conspiracy hides behind our love!

At night in the border where the snow falls where the snow isn't falling the concept of love the limits of love the mass of love one by one stood under the guillotine of time

Following the sandy air covered with loneliness, the heads of love were roughly chopped off Like the hats of a desert that had finished a duel they accelerated betrayal to leave the border where the snow falls

And the lovers who had been divided in two remained

White snow ... falls

Viera Vola[6] stops her song
and stares vacantly out the window
without even loading her typewriter with paper
I am the way of the border you live on
A night where white birds tuck in their ankles and unfurl the light
the white birch forest slowly turns ashen
snow falls and my psychic reading
where snow is falling
for the first time in one hundred years
is a round stain

NOTES

1) The name of an instrumental piece by an unknown composer that was included only within black market copies of *Border's Night*, which was

created during a gathering of third-world musicians mourning the passing of parrot gypsy Viera Viola.

2) According to the association Astrologers Without Borders, this now-difficult-to-find book on teacup fortune-telling divulged in detail how to use the shape and color of tea stains at the bottom of a cup to tell fortunes and even reveal the secrets to romance; at the time, it was considered required reading for teenage girls and boys.

3) He borrowed his name from Wilde Oscar, an explorer known as "Tough Oscar," but only his name. He has no other relationship with the other man. However, one cannot deny that he was influenced by the gracefulness of Dorian Grays, who appears in his posthumous work *Border as a Fantasy*.

4) This name is brought from the exact name of Jean Marco Genet, the diary thief that appears in "Border of Innocence" in Wilde Oscar's debut work *Border as a Fantasy*. I jot down as I sing: the song that Jean Marco Genet sings in the work while crossing the border, "My Innocence Is Only Proved through Depravity," made a deep impression on me.

5) The feeling of inebriation was borrowed from a bar in an alleyway of Milon. It is said that Gabriel Garcia Vaquez's family, at this place, received loneliness instead of money for their alcohol for one hundred years, and even now, this place is disappearing as a safe house for the artists who have crossed the border.

6) A diva born and raised in a tiny gypsy village in Bohemia, Czech Republic. She is called the big parrot of gypsy music for her deep voice which she mastered as she crossed thousands of borders.

The Last Person on Space Ferris Wheel No. 12*

The blizzard conquered the city by surprise. The people of the city had fled in desperation to avoid the army attack of pumpkin-sized snowflakes, but the blizzard had marched in swiftly and turned the city silent like a war widow. In the absence of church bells ringing or cars honking or the sound of the morning reveille, stillness made a tour of the city for the first time in a long while. Only the occasional wind gently disturbed this silent landscape.

The city turned into a huge snow tomb. The people of the city hibernated** without a word. Everchanging days and nights came and went like the soft crunch of snow. The blizzard gradually lost its roar. Over and over, as the tomb melted and chafed under the sun and wind, it created an air of decisiveness.

Twenty-eight months later,* a red piece of Space Ferris Wheel No. 12 emerged like the lips of a tomboy. It was a sense of vitality granted to a world that had its mouth heavily shut. Holding a mouthful of light for a moment, it grew long and then opened its mouth wide with an *ahhhh*. It was the first gateway to the new city.

After passing through the gate that was surrounded by an unknown silence, a fat man who had made a show of hanging icicles silently appeared. The man waddled out and looked around, his body swaying from one side to another. The man's nearly dead, absentmindedly frozen penis, hanging over his pants and underwear that were gathered at his ankles, went about and came around, as though seeking out a called shot in life, like Babe Ruth's** bat.

The world was cold-hearted. The man stiffly controlled the expression on his face. He was unable to easily move his pale feet and was stuck in place. He thought about the habit of people who turned into objects. He reminisced about nights of countless amusement parks and masturbation. Those were warm days. The man closed his eyes. His frozen eyelids did not come down. The man went back into the space ferris wheel. He locked the door. It was a friendly, antisocial time. The man stared unflinchingly at the fatso reflected in the frozen chair opposite him. In the cozy space of the space ferris wheel, the fat man was about to burst out laughing as he always had. Soon, the man gave into the dream he had cherished for a long time. Snowstorms covered with white curtains drove the city back behind the ghosts.

NOTES

* The title of a picture drawn at the last entrance of Ghost City. The picture had the following words scribbled on it: "That night, a man stepped into Space Ferris Wheel No. 12 alone. He was a fat man who resembled American actor John Goodman, and I could easily guess why he had come all the way to this ghost town to sit in the Space Ferris Wheel. The man was a city man." The night I came across this drawing and note, I was the last person there.

* This refers to an animal that flies through the winter, limiting its metabolic activity to as low as possible. While most humans do not hibernate, there are some who hibernate with their heads shoved into the gaps of their souls.

* A film directed by Danny Boy, released on January 11, 2111. It is about the trauma of the survivors of the city where the White Virus disappeared. The film faced controversy for its final scene, in which humans who gave up on being humans fell into silence and sleep.

* The legendary "King of Home Runs" in American Major League Baseball. On October 1, 1932, during game 3 of the World Series between the New York Yankees and the Chicago Cubs, he hit the baseball in the direction he had pointed, creating the legend of the "called shot." The legend has also been made into a film starring American actor John Goodman.

Write the Novel, the Novel; in the Final Days
of the Novel, Blake with the Blue Gloves

Blake, who had entered his final days, was already enraptured by all kinds of fictions.[1]

—Are you ready to order?

After he started tripping on the novelist's psychedelic, Blake expanded his consciousness.[2] Blake thought of a small, dark nanny. Soon, the screen covered in Batang font grew transparent. On snowy nights, large, white breasts always appeared inside the glass coffin.

The lid of the coffin opened.[3] Blake sucked on the left nipple of the drinking doll, which was giving off an artificial kind of beauty. Blue gloves gushed forth. Though they were poor quality chemicals, the blue gloves soothed Blake's broken heart.

The novelist observed today's protagonist from an omniscient writer's point of view. The scene was unstable. It was an aftereffect of the LSD. The novelist adjusted the drinking doll's mammary cable. Blake stuffed the whole blue gloves into his mouth and melted down the Korean-made sofa. The novelist parted the drinking doll's lips like they did in fanfics.

Sing, sweet lad.

You will turn into a shining star.

The one and only star on this national planet.

The drinking doll's voice resounded in the final days. Blake raised his body.[4] The novelist closed the drinking doll's lips and waited for Blake's reaction. Blake stared into the drinking doll's lifeless pupils. Blake gradually acquired all narrative archetypes.

In the cupboard with the vanished pattern / I discovered her blue gloves / Old possessions that had been pressed down à la Francis Jammes / When she went / and put on the blue gloves and fell asleep / moss flourished in her dream / therefore I am warm and not lonely / Stroking the snow white face of death / I recited a poem that ends beautifully / But now / where could those lace-adorned blue gloves have gone / The ones that let my dead self rest in peace / since summer that year / And we lost blue poems and

Blake caressed the stiff barrel of the gun. He sucked hard on the drinking doll's right nipple. The blue gloves rode Blake's chin and fell to the ground. Blake watched his ground for a long while. It was something possible only during his final days.

—Are you ready to finish up?

The novelist pressed the button for the psychedelic. LSD's magnetic field recovered its equilibrium. The scene was calm. With a sense of déjà vu, Blake read the blue gloves that were written on the ground in shorthand. Once again, the novelist operated the psychedelic.

—Are you ready to finish up?

Blake and snowy nights always passed through the glass coffin. The lid was shut. Blake caressed the drinking doll's cheek. He felt a kind of warmth that humans can't have. Blake pulled out paper and pen and whispered.[5]

The trigger was pulled. In those final days, Blake completed the blue glove. The novelist hit "Enter" to deal with his small story. The glass coffin was slowly deleted following the space bar. The novelist sucked the breast and looked at the dead face. It was a face created by mankind. The screen turned off with a ray of light.

Blake slowly came out of Blake and in those final days Blake looked at the blue gloves and left the final days.

NOTES

1) "Séverine, Séverine, Séverine."
2) "Blue gloves, blue gloves, blue gloves."
3) "Now there are no more women with small, dark breasts."
4) "You have a more Séverine-esque voice than Séverine."
5) "Séverine and Séverine, I dedicate all of myself to you two. I hope you always keep going, Séverine, cheers to you, Séverine. For her life which would be so much gentler and happier without me in it. I LOVE YOU, I LOVE YOU!"

The Tale of Cho[1]

Once upon a time, there was a man with a surname Cho (初) in No Village. Laboriously tolerating the funerals of those who had vanished, Cho lived. No one knew the past of Cho from A to Z. Only rumors ran rampant. Many gossips became the song's lyrics. Spinning and spinning and spinningspinningspinning, people sang about the time when Cho studied one stroke of reckless poop under the flying chickadee and perfected his delivering technique (傳法) at the Ipseol Pavilion (入雪亭).[2] The song made the dream come true.

In the conception dream of Grandma Chatty, who gave birth at the age of seventy, Cho's pestle stirred the snowfield in the shape of "五入" and fetched the white kois pouring out from a penis like Bak Daekidaeki waterfall. So, after the interpretation that is more generous than its dream is given, to see Cho's deceased penis, people of all different kinds stampeded, following Cho's outstanding stream of urine.

Anyhow. One day, the great water of four rivers leaked into No Village. A swarm of rats appeared. Grasshoppers rained. Cho examined the shape, width and volume of the water. The water was dead. Cho hung a ground mouse head bait on the blue funeral lantern for missing people. Rattling, he left home. No Village people crowded into the river's deep-set eyes. The moon fell over. Darkness flooded. Empty houses sank one by one.

A cow's empty skin was floating, a pig's empty skin was floating, a chicken's empty skin was floating, and a human's empty skin was floating, and the funeral lights that were lighting up the cheeks were hung one by one on the surface of water. A dark alley of water glittered with blue fire drops. The gentle wind wrote a congratulatory message (祝文) on the water. Along the edge of the scandal, all the junks from underwater No Village took off their skin and sat in a circle. Lords Caught Fish, who retired from Heaven and made great progress with their scamming techniques, also crawled out to taste Cho's baits, shouting, "It costs money to make money."

Cho pulled out his penis and got it hard while saying goodbye to the last funeral lights and understanding the hidden intention of propitious mourning (好喪). He drew "五入." *Dun-dun-wah-wah-wah*, he sang one of the forty-four songs in *Delivering Technique* (傳法).[3]

As they drink exorcist liquor, Cheeky egg ghosts frown and squat on the grass and mess around with the thick members of the men who wet their pants with bold streams. Virgin ghosts share a jar of grain wine on good terms and, standing up in a row, open their black vaginas and vigorously pass cow blood until the universe's ears turn blue. Ha, the Spirits of the rivers, whose appetites have increased after a long time, smack their lips and move their fins to create the path for funeral lights. The dead water of No Village surges here and the underwater and overwater moons are formed. The night is split in two, and disappearing people and animals sent back.

The sound of Cho melted into the water. Daekidaeki Bak Daekidaeki white snow streamed down. The gaping heads of the underwater creatures all lifted and grew hard at the same time in order to see Cho's penis. Only then did the *Samsin* sisters rub their sleepy eyes and organize the records of blessings *badumdumdumdum*.

Later, No Village people opened and closed their gills as they watched the underwater moon, saying that was the day the head of a doomed mouse was cut off; that was the day each *Samsin* sister received a box of rice cake manufactured by the overwater moon rabbit for their first night shift allowance; that was the day when the two-hundred-year-old Grandma Chatty, without a husband, conceived a baby who looks just like her husband; that was the old day when Cho, the sterile character (字) of No Village, went missing.

NOTES

1) This is based on the first draft that was transmitted through the song that was often sung in No Village. The lyrics consist of the last conception dream of the Chatty grandmother of No Village, who had twelve late children. However, this story and song became extinct a long time ago.

2) A pavilion that was in the Surim Temple of No Village. It is told that the snow was piled up firmly to build it. Currently, the pavilion is no longer there, and only a part of the training mantra engraved on the glans of the pavilion is handed down. The mantra goes as follows: "That night, heavy snow came endlessly, and heavy snowstorms fiercely raged. Dharma did not move even as he was snowed on. The morning dawned. Dharma looked at Dharma standing in the snow and said nothing."

3) A collection of the song lyrics sung by student monks at the Surim temple as they waited for the snow to pile up to their knees. Human life and death were described like in a dream. It is told that the bound book was dissolved in water.

Mansion

y Taïaut

One day
I passed by a place
that had disappeared.⁾

Those lost years
we had been magnificent boys.

Searching for the dead
on stone steps where time had broken
we used to kiss.

Where could those young ghosts have gone?

I stopped in my tracks at the place with the iron gate
where the sphinx was cracking with rust.

I saw a large dog
plodding through the garden all alone
like a butler who cannot abandon his family's crest.

It was Grenier.

Grenier
did not recognize me.

Perhaps, then, Greniere was not Grenier.

A sudden rain
hung low along the uphill road
that Greniere climbed.

Miraculously the rain
f o r   a   m o m e n t
restored the garden
that promised a soul.

Sunshine forms a community of friendship.
Plants grow green, their pinkies locked.
The mansion is surrounded by a shadowy corridor.
We nestle up to the blue bones and fall asleep.

For a moment
the mirage that escaped the rain disappeared.
The rain stopped.

Where did Grenier go?

Here
on the other side of the broken windows
with the heaps of small black stones
we achieved a wish tower.

We heaped up the blood.
The blood-colored stones collapsed.
This is humanity's history of love.

Time, taking time,
demolishes everything.

From the far-off cemetery,
Grenier gazed down
with the shadow of a crucifix his mouth.⁾

Grenier,
as if he had discovered an old acquaintance
faintly barked.

I,
ignoring the cries clinging to those degenerating vocal cords,
passed through the back door of the mansion
for the government.

Like a hole piercing through a steel helmet
time widened.

I couldn't ever come back here
alive.

If so,
if it is because I'm dead.

Around the time of war and peace
we were already
in unison
calling me a dead person
from the mansion where no one disappears.⁾

NOTES

☽ I cannot testify to the mansion. Around that time, I began to lose my hearing. Around that time, the days of the two boys who used the empty house as a playground were over. Around that time, many dogs were beaten to death. Around that time, according to ears that could hear, the dog days began. Around that time, I used to think of the two boys who fell asleep, hiding in the chapel and covered in plants. The two boys used to smile peacefully, tying a red ribbon to my tail.

☽ I cannot pay attention to the boy. Around that time, I began to lose my sight. Around that time, the wish towers that protected the mansion collapsed. Around that time, many dogs were preyed upon. Around that time, according to eyes that could see, the most doggone of dog days could be seen. Around that time, I used to think of a boy who killed a soul, hiding in a graveyard and covered in fire and water. The boy used to bark, pointing fingers at the red ribbon on my tail.

☽ Faintly. I cannot get away from the voice. Around that time, voices began to occur. Around that time, a boy's stones were heaped up. Around that time, many dogs began to wander about. Around that time, according to a voice that was blurting out, the undogged days, with neither beginning nor end. Around that time, I strolled through a black corridor, was swept away in my dream, and heard a boy who promised his soul to another boy. The boy used to borrow voices, tying a red ribbon to my tail.

The party was dying. Susan set up several silvery serenities. The sound brightened up. Susan slowly waved a match. Mitchell, who took charge of music in *Sur Le Jadis*, played a long guitar to call back memories. For the first time, Susan looked at ginger-hair Chichi who, dejected, followed Ron Wood. Today's Mitchell began to sing in the voice of the past Mitchell. The light grew. Tonight, I know fake people who couldn't fall asleep. Juno Temple, Wes Bentley, Hank Azaria, Bobby Cannavale, Adam Brody, Robert Patrick, James Franco, Eric Roberts, Romeo Brown, Susan Boreman, and Linda, Linda, Linda who's more human-like than them. Eric Roberts, who invariably plays a drunk visitor in *Melted Down*,[1] turned his drug-assisted face to Linda.

He ludicrously opened his silicone-containing industrial lips.

—Look, it's Julia's million-dollar smile.

Bobby Cannavale consoled him.

—It's okay. Your life is worth twenty dollars.

Robert Patrick opened his money cli . . .

— Time to open your lips.

Wes Bentley shouted.

—Let's all make a bet on this legendary throat.

Adam Brody recited the lines.

—Love, harder, harder, even harder.

Hank Azaria announced his opening speech.

—Here, I brought this for our last moment.

Applause broke out rhythmically.

—Mitchell, I need more *Sur Le Jadis*

Juno Temple asked him calmly. *This is the last party we prepared for you. Show us your light. Susan, you're gonna blow us in one shot. With the power you and only you have. Believe in the love God has given you and only you.* For a moment, Susan stopped the friendly acclamations of naked bodies.

Susan brought the dildo used in *Sur Le Jadis*. Seventeen minutes, twenty-two minutes, twenty-seven minutes . . . Unfeigned acclamations of fake people sprayed its vaginal discharge. Susan opened her mouth. Deep within her throat, the silences that made up Susan circulated through her respiratory tract. Then, silence going in and out was added as the component of a night. Susan raised the seventeen-minute dildo. It was a boring start that suited the start of a bet. Every time Susan inserted a dildo in order, Mitchell tore and tied the strings of the long guitar and rendered long, beautiful, short and boring tremors. Susan thought about her old times every five centimeters. It was already late.

But life is always already late. The voice of Today's Mitchell formed in his eyes of the past. Timely, Susan arrived at Hank's thing. She raised her hands over her head. *Hank, I can't swallow this.* Susan was disappointed with Susan. *Only you can swallow this. Who else could swallow this if it weren't you? Susan, Susan, Susan,* Susan kept calling Susan out. *It's your retirement party today. It's time to show what a retirement party is. We're waiting for you.* Susan hummed Mitchell's last song about the old times. *Don't be late, I think we too should go to sleep now.* People surrounding Susan started to fall to death as if they were asleep. At that time, the Earth was at a power outage.

Susan called Hank Azaria's thing. *Lovelace.* The fire built on the stillness was shaken out. Today, Susan's song for Mitchell was finally over. Susan swallowed till the end. All the fire crumbled. It was a refreshing early morning. The gunshot went straight, penetrating through the silence. The window broke. It was a hit. The content of the silence that forms a night dropped low. An automated answering machine operated. *Susan, I am truly honored to be your last man. This retirement party will be a killer.* Romeo Brown was intoxicated with a predictable universe[2] again today. Susan put the lovelace down on the table. Susan floated into the bedroom, dragging a home dress with a discolored imitation pearl. Linda, barely stepping on the edge of Susan's clothes with her four feet, followed her in short and quick steps. During the long time when she was climbing up to her bedroom, Susan looked around at the faceless faces that chanted Susan. Shaking a dildo, Susan memorized oily lines. *Penetrate me with a stronger one, please.* Susan opened the bedroom door. Ron Wood and Chichi were sleeping like a log on her bed. Susan approached the back of Chichi and clung her skull to her crumpled back and dented buttocks. She hugged Chichi. Ron Wood opened his eyes and looked into Susan's eyes. Chichi opened her eyes and looked into Ron Wood's eyes. Susan closed her eyes and looked into Ron Wood's eyes. James Franco, who had fallen asleep somewhere, shouted

Susan like the first of the gang to die on the Threesome island.[3)]
Susan! Susan! Susan! Where are you gone? Today's a retirement party
for the Los Angeles Angel. Oh gosh, you can't fall asleep like this. It was
a night where the remainder of the wick that is burned black was
short. The party was over. Linda carefully pushed the bedroom door
shut.

NOTES

1) During the nintey-minute running time of the movie, many people
surrounding a person, many people surrounding a person, many people
surrounding a person, many people surrounding a person appear one by
one and bestow abundant white lonelinesses on a person's black loneli-
ness. When white liquid runs down and stains the black screen, the trans-
parent faces of the characters that have appeared so far appear and mingle
their expressions with one another as they shake. This last welcome scene
is indeed gangbang-esque.

2) Colorless, tasteless, and odorless white powder. Though it causes tolerance
and psychological dependency, it does not cause physical withdrawal. The
main effects of powder are a montage, overlap, jump cut, flashback, long
take, etc.

3) The movie featuring the journey of reenactors who came to the Three-
some island for a trip. The main story is about one person combined into
two, one person combined into two, and one person combined into two.
The last farewell scenes—in which one-persons who became two-peoples
sit around and observe one another disappear—form a group.

What Do Angels Do on Silent and Holy Nights;
Unfortunately for dear Mr. Pale Blue Eyes, several
~~criticities of Mr. Pale Blue Eyes's manuscript do not~~
align with the proclivities of the Velvet Underground
Theater troupe, so we are sending back parts of the
manuscript and will endeavor to send back the rest,
which was misplaced by Mr. Lou Reed, once it is found
(the curtain rises, the stage is empty)[1]

☾

Michael With the Black Naked Body is in the middle of reception with an erection, and holding a hard, thick whip When the oak wall clock chimes, Michael turns and heads to the second floor It is stairless and the neckless ghosts' breaths follow along rays of light, nodding nodding as it flows out Michael cowers back back breathing the ghosts' breaths in and out, blurring and sharpening over and over.

☾

Michael Who Passed Through the Long Narrow Corridor-like Darkness stands at the door of a shattered forest Michael, rubbing his variable eyes uncontrollably, exists without a doubt As the Gabriel Crayon plants in the forest lie prone like dogs beside overgrown wallpaper, their completely naked heads raised stiffly, looking out the window, Michael, holding his breath, enters the forest As he enters, Michael's heart pierces through the darkness, Gabriel, and the window in that order

Winterbilledwhitebirds come with snow in their beaks Snowflakes both fake and real fall When it snows, Forest, who would knock on the window with a palm small and thin like three-thirty in the morning, is nowhere to be seen Michael leads the way forward, forward, caressing his whip, and shifts his gaze toward the dead light surrounding Gabriel's crumpled back.

It's time to leave

Michael thinks out loud *This will be the last time* Michael thinks as if out loud

Forest

Michael intones and thinks Michael, thinks He strikes Gabriel's rear with his whip A dark spot blooms vividly on Gabriel's buttock Gabriel growls and twists his body around Gabriel drops the leash he was holding tightly in his teeth Michael brandishes the warm whip three or four more times With his own mouth, Michael speaks as he thinks.

Woof woof, Gabriel barks woof woof
Woof woof, Michael barks woof woof
Woof woof, Forest barks woof woof

They bark together good-naturedly Michael lets go of the whip he was holding The whip stays floating in the air Like a black stem standing upright, Michael drops to his knees Gabriel hunkers forward like typhoid Michael strokes Gabriel's blood Gabriel strokes Michael's knees Vanishing and staying in the light, Forest—looking down at Michael and Gabriel, hovering by them, stroking their lips—rises up little by little.

It is a gloomy night and the angels think as they converse

They look like lumps of meat
Humans are lumps of meat
Would this be what the touch of death feels like
What would humans do last night?

A flock of bright bell tolls, which almost seem visible, unfurl their white wings and descend upon the forest where Forest died In the dim pocket of light, as Michael into his crotch—Gabriel into his crotch—pushes Gabriel's head—pushes Michael's head, Michael and Gabriel speak.

Merry Christmas, Buddha

145

Michael and Gabriel gaze at each other's pale blue nights for a long time Forest now appears and, gazing in wonder at the silver snowflakes, taps *tick tock tick tock* on the window with a faint finger.[2]

NOTES

1) Fur-clad Venus, who arrived in Velvet's underground, is currently disappearing to write the curtain-raiser "Pale Blue Eyes" for the play *Pale Blue Eyes*.

2) (The stage is still empty and the curtain falls) Not long after the incident, when they had vanished without a trace, some said they left with their wings cut up into black mini-minis. Some said they saw them unfurling their fully grown wings and flying up into the sky. But most said, "You want me to believe they're angels?" saying that everything had been a lie from the start. And today, as I disappear, listening to the Velvet Underground, writing "Pale Blue Eyes," I grow curious. What do angels do on those silent and holy nights?

Sad Vagina[1]

The night disappeared. Darkness persisted. Jinsu finally chose Mrs. Emmanuel as his first prey. She's old enough to die. She lives alone. Though at a dying age, she lives alone and never meets anyone. After contemplation, Jinsu wanted to kill the humiliation he had felt when he saw her.

Having lived by herself for a long time, Mrs. Emmanuel's body was frugal. There was not much flesh to gnaw off her baked neck, and her thickly sliced forearm couldn't fill a single bone china plate. Her thighs, which he thought would have some meat to eat, smelled like a stale fish. So stale that he couldn't eat it without pinching his nose. Fortunately, the lump of darkness she had nurtured inside her breast reminded him of a normal dinner.

Jinsu took off his bloodstained T-shirt and pressed his deficient night vision goggles on the observation hole. The black figures of the black figures who were dragging black figures formed parts of the night. The cannibalism started as they each saw fit. A wild night for surviving to the last has dawned. Sluggishly, Jinsu headed to the secret room in the basement of the basement.[2]

Jean glared at Jinsu without hiding animosity. In silence, Jinsu put down the plate of prey in front of Jean. Jean twisted his body painfully when he smelled the prey. Jean's appetites, full of hatred and viler than those of beasts, had grown even more ferocious in the past several days.

Jinsu lay down on the mattress and turned toward the wall. Someone would have eaten it anyway.[3] Jinsu closed his eyes, feeling full and fatigued at the same time. The light was fluttering over the window. Through the crease of light, someone was looking down at them quietly. Where the light was blown away was Mrs. Emmanuel. She was standing there, naked. A faultlessly white vagina was there, looking at his cold naked body, handcuffed and barking under Jean's crotch.

It burst out. Coughing, Jinsu stroked the lump of darkness stuck in the pit of his stomach. The shame didn't go away. It wasn't meant to go away from the start. We were humans. Jinsu held his breath. The low cry of Jean, who's sucking and ripping Mrs. Emmanuel's fingers, loitered through the night.

NOTES

1) The title of a handmade picture book by a female writer Manon, who appeared in the French literary circles in the late eighteenth century and then soon disappeared. This handmade picture book, which only has one copy, was burnt by her lover Emmanuel, but the picture of a vagina, the only picture that luckily survived in fire is now kept in the wellspring of Manon.

2) "As peace returned to the village, Emmanuel began building a secret room somewhere in his body to prepare for death. People called the secret room in the basement 'wellspring.'"—the complete text of Manon's novel *Vagina*.

3) What Emmanuel said in the Virginia court in defense of his cannibalism, after chopping, frying, and eating his lover Manon. Later, this became the talk of the people who eat human flesh again and again.

A Mechanic of the Night[1]

An automat restaurant on Greenwich local road where the sun had disappeared out of orbit. Dressed in a soiled maintenance uniform, Raymond's reddened face was cast with the deep inner side of the night. Raymond's toolbox on the table turned the night's loneliness into a still life.

Raymond peeled off the silver wrapper of Uncle's Burger and took a bite of the hamburger. A k.d. lang–looking[2] man in leather pants left the restaurant, scanning Raymond. Raymond turned his head and looked out the window. The man's back, captured by the moonlight, was thin and artless. The man turned around and bit sorrow. A man approached the man who was emitting smoke. Raymond recognized at a glance that the man in the worn Levi jeans and a shabby tool belt was Humphrey, a plumber living on the Morning Sun road.

Humphrey and his wife Virginia used to call Raymond regularly to repair parts of their often-loose heads and hearts. It was always midnight, and Virginia served a blueberry pie every time Raymond fixed her heart. Her fingers were tinged with dark violet, like the beak of a dead bird.

A piece of wet lettuce from the hamburger fell onto Raymond's thigh. Chewing at the stiff beef patty, Raymond gazed at the men's cold and sour shadows. Two shadows, like ghost sailors who help sail through the night, glided into the public bathroom where the Pierre and Jules[3] billboard had been installed.

In the distance, holograms rose from the graves of the broken mechanical humans. The paintings of Edward Hopper,[4] whose light and darkness had flown away, were projected.[5] No more words were necessary for this midnight. Raymond left the restaurant that constitutes the third part of the night. He passed through dead machines and hopped into an old gasoline truck. He started the engine. The truck's turn signal flickered toward the road that stretched into the cemetery and then soon went out.

NOTES

1) "My painting series of night people cannot escape his magnetic field. This is because, during the time I spent most of my childhood, his replicated painting was the "the painting of a barbershop," which anyone on the asteroid of abandoned mechanical humans could easily see whenever and wherever. Without much determination." See "A Conversation with the Author I" in the free art newspaper *Collage*.

2) Canadian-born country singer-songwriter.—Translator

3) The two artists combine photographs and paintings in collaboration. While kitschily meshing a ship in the sea, a movie, sailors, movie stars, exotic customs, space, eroticism, gay culture, love and death, they cross the boundary between illusion and reality and bring out fantasies about artificial space.—Translator

4) An American painter. His works include "Automat," "Gas," "Nighthawks," and "Morning Sun."—Translator

5) "I got a clue about this work at a restaurant on the corner of Greenwich road. There, I unconsciously saw the loneliness of a big city," Edward Hopper said. And I'll have to say, "Whenever I saw his paintings, I thought of the night of unconsciously abandoned mechanical men." See "A Conversation with the Author II" in the free art newspaper *Collage*.

He was floating in suspended black-and-white. Different parts of his naked mind, darkened by soggy Mongolian spots.

Pulling his red oxide hat down low, Montgomery broke away from the edge of the sunset. He stood in front of the black-and-white that spanned the forest, swallowing water and fog. He adjusted his pupils. A human was floating. A distinct human, who makes the light-and-dark move back with his mystical skin. Montgomery set up an old model of a New Generation antenna, then sat down on a great face stone on the verge of disappearing and bent over. He opened his left hand. He wiped the lines of his palm clean. He pulled off the cellulanamic nail of his right index finger. He started to write a letter. Only then did Montgomery look like a one-of-a-kind machine. Flying saucer crickets flew in as they dyed the evening sky in thirds with purple ion gas.

Dear Mr. Hudson,

At last, I found a human at the edges of this sunset that is endlessly cleaved in two. But the human is not alive. Perhaps there is no one alive left on Earth. Do you remember the light of humans? Even in the depleted black-and-white, the dead are radiant and beautiful. Is that what the love of humans is?

Between Montgomery's lips, white, Montgomery opened his mouth. White, and he pushed his nails in. Whitely, he folded and unfolded his palm. The fate line in his palm returned with the damp fog. There was no way to tell whether the transmission had been successful. Montgomery opened his leather bag. He opened his bosom. He opened his heart. He replaced the dead battery with a dead battery. Montgomery flattened the nose of the dead battery. The lights of the fireflies flickered on. *Of all the cognocardioergonomic nature we've created, these lights are the one bearable thing.* Montgomery watched the fluttering, trembling song for a long time. He thought of Mr. Hudson's gentle eyes when he sent off the humans. Montgomery switched his body to sleep mode. He swallowed the last human-emotion capsule. He took out a collection of poetry by some philosopher. A night like an open page took shape.

We will look back on the civilization of love
someday buried deep
in winter night's love
At last when the place where the congelation of
the mystery of life we had broken
from near and far
close and apart
together and alone
askew and straight on
melted cleanly away
So now

Open your arms and embrace me, Montgomery whispered. He decided to go to sleep. Montgomery had wakeful eyes. His black-

and-white sleep was covered with Mongolian spots that had escaped the human mind. As he turned over the pages, Montgomery either fell asleep or did not. Montgomery himself did not know. A moving picture of two humans with their cheeks pressed together was stuck in the middle of a public plaza. They pulled their cheeks apart and held hands. They let go of their hands and bit each other's lips. They dropped each other's lips and turned around. They turned, and walked away. The picture stopped. They had turned against each other forever.

Montgomery closed the book. *Mr. Hudson, is this the sadness of humans?* A blurry hologram ☽ appeared above Montgomery's head. The howls of a wolf rang out precisely twelve times without fail. Montgomery's eyes closed with a rattle. Only then did Montgomery, with his eyes closed, come to feel that he was a dying mechanical man in search of Montgomery Clift. Montgomery's body grew cold. Above the wreckage of a love hotel, where faraway winter's night had fallen, two human corpses locked in an embrace melted into a puddle.#

NOTES

The following was written to laboriously hide Montgomery Clift, who appears in "Montgomery Clift," a lesser-known story in a relatively unknown sci-fi short-story collection titled *A Story Consisting of Seven Machines*. Therefore, this mind will automatically blow up inside your mind in ten seconds.

10, 9, 8, 7, 6, 5, 4, 3, 2, 1.

Montgomery Clift is now truly just about anywhere in you.

Earth[1)]

A blue eye finally stood still in the front yard of the monastery[2)] that has a narrow cheek. The castle, darkened as the last ink bottle collapsed, was as silent as a cassette tape played to the end.[3)] The blue eye pulled up the electric current from its little toe. Like a long, painted giraffe on the brink of sinking, its eyelashes plunged and went up. The eye sparkled once again. The blue eye stealthily rotated 360 degrees. Anywhere it lit up, only manholes with the closed test card curtain were there. The blood vessels in the blue eye snapped one by one and emanated flames. Each time, the whole castle flickered. In the pile of ashes where the light began to fade in solitude, the blue eye finally acknowledged that it was the last insignificant streetlight[4)] of this place. With automatic technology, the blue eye disassembled the castle's thinnest and longest single bridge, from which the anthology's sheath was metaphorically peeling. Over the monastery yard where the horoscope scripture is engraved, the disjointed bridges piled up in a rhyming couplet like an altar. The blue eye, soaring alone, sang to a cosmos spider's cobweb and lit up its final gaze. With black smoke, the blue eye turned off dimly. Black-and-white tears fluttered in flames. Hundreds of millions of eyelash holograms rose to the sky each moment.

The cosmos spider turned its eight rocket legs toward the planet's archives, the place that had vanished, loading its butthole with the eyelashes that had been stuck in the cobweb. When the ash-grey cobweb cleared, a flock of Transyl-white-butterfly-cabbage worms[5] swarmed in and began to nibble on the planet where lights ~~were out.~~

NOTES

1) One of the planets in the solar system; human beings lived there. It circled along the third orbit from solitude, with the moon as a satellite. Since the thin, transparent magnetic field covering the planet neared solitude, it began to develop a pitch-black hole.

2) Had once been a place where monks or nuns led a communal life under a set of disciplines, it became a place where the cloned replicas and cyborgs who are about to expire led a communal life under a set of silence, waiting for death. Each day, mass and communion were held under the guidance of the head monk, who is elected according to its expiration date. They learned aesthetics through philosophy and mathematics and wrote poetry through labor. The monastery had a library, a theater, a hospital ward, and a graveyard, thereby allowing them to be self-sufficient.

3) "A small glass box equipped with an emotion tape to record emotions. It was developed by Philips of the Netherlands in xx63 and used for a long time, but as the use of emotions became unnecessary, it could not be auto-reversed and thus disappeared." See *The Archives for Lost Things*.

4) A lighting equipment installed along a street for the safety and security of traffic until the multi-function streetlight robot was developed in xx68. Different streetlights were used depending on the location of the installation. There were various types of poles, including the artist type with a bent tip, the mathematician type with lamps hanging from the branches,

which were spreading horizontally from the tip, and the philosopher type with the lamps hanging from the head of the pole.

5) The larvae of Vania-cabbage-white butterflies. Their bodies are light brown, and they have fine hair densely coming out of their surfaces. Vania-cabbage-white-butterflies lay yellowish eggs at the speed of 1 centimeter per second once every Hierro in the Galactic Ecclesiastical Calendar. As the eggs turn light green, they become caterpillars. The grown larvae gnaw at a withered planet and pull out the Transyl from its mouth, bind themselves and become pupae.

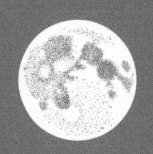

The Real Queer Sci-fi–Metafiction Theater:
A Handbook to *Glory Hole*

PARK SANG SOO

Welcome!

I bet it's the first time you've ever read a poetry collection like this.

I wish I could see your face right now. You might be feeling frustrated, or very confused. Maybe you applauded the collection as you were reading it. Or you might have thought that each verse had too much information, packed as they were with characters, events, and emotions, but with origins that were hard to pinpoint. There was a subtext to almost every poem, but even that was only halfway implied or entirely disguised. If we tried to grasp each poem together with its subtext, it would easily take over an hour to read. What is more, each poem is like a Möbius strip, reflecting one itself endlessly, as would a hall of mirrors. Footnotes or endnotes, too, appear incessantly, impeding reading speed while expanding the scope of each poem indefinitely. *So how on earth should I read these poems?* you might be wondering. I imagine some of you rushed to the commentary because you were seeking an answer.

If you find yourself nodding, then let me ask you something. Is this book a collection of poems or stories? Is it sci-fi, pornography, hard-core *yaoi*, or fanfiction? If it is none of these, is it a lovingly crafted history report on the pop- and sub-cultures of English-speaking countries in the 1950s and 1960s? Or is it a special homage to the American beat and hippie writers of the same period? Could it be a satirical allegory of corruption and political power, or is it a teen drama wherein characters go on road trips in search of their true selves? What if we consider that the style and sensibility of these poems resemble that of translated poetry? Or that new characters appear every time you turn the page? Or that the poems themselves have a distinct apocalyptic, dystopian vibe?

These are rhetorical questions, but everything I have said so far describes this lively body of work. If you happen to have a degree of empathy for—or prior knowledge about—the world like this, you will find no other composition as interesting or unique as this one. It will reawaken and revitalize the nerd within you, hyperlinking to the background knowledge you revived; and you will feel a thrill as your knowledge reassembles into a unique kind of melancholy and an intellectual suspense.

If you lack this context, then you will need to put in a bit of extra effort from now on. Those of you who find this collection challenging at times yet cannot let go of its immense appeal—those of you who *almost* understand and find yourself growing more interested—try creating a central narrative that brings together the collection's numerous fictional accounts. Make an effort to do this as you keep reading. Come up with your own hypotheses, shifting away from the main narrative and developing new ones. Now, let us try to develop our narrative based on three keywords: "queer," "sci-fi," and "metafiction."

"Glory Hole": The Start of Queer Sensitivity

Sexual minorities made their appearance in Korean poetry for the first time in 2005, with a character named "Sikoku, the Man Dressed as a Woman" from Hwang Byungsng's first book of poetry. The "Man Dressed as a Woman" character often exhibited confusion about their gender identity, vacillating between male and female. Hwang's characterization depicted the pretentious, violent backdrop of heterosexual relationships, as well as the superficiality of the world, as intense feelings of disgust and shame.

On the other hand, Kim Hyun specifically chooses to create gay characters. Those who are not interested in LGBTQ issues may skim through many parts of his poems. But for those who care even just a little, this collection is a remarkable, first-of-its-kind achievement built upon extraordinary gay sensibility.

Even the title is sensational. *Geulori Hol* might be the name of a hotel reception hall or a wedding hall, but not always.[2] In fact, "glory hole" is a slang associated with gay male culture—it refers to a hole in the partition between the cubicles of a public restroom. Gay men would enter different cubicles on either side of the hole, through which they could watch each other masturbate, peep on one another, and perform oral sex.[3] In Korea, glory holes were

2 [In Korean transliteration, "hole" and "hall" are written and pronounced the same (홀, *hol*).—Suhyun J. Ahn and Archana Madhavan]

3 Chingusai, *Gay Culture Holic* (Seoul: Cine21 Books, 2011), p. 267. I will refer to this book for further explanations of gay culture. [See also Alessa

occasionally found in public toilets, until the gay community started becoming more visible; now, they are almost all gone. With that in mind, can any title be more secret, or explicit, than this one?

Let us look at "Old Baby Homo," the twenty-sixth of the fifty-one poems. We will learn that the title of this poem was not randomly chosen. We will also discern the underlying structure dominating this collection.

> The tattered night when we wear a wig with sausage curls and drink fetid beer, I sing unintelligibly. For the sake of the buddies who shot a rocket beyond the boy's orbit before the countdown was over. Goodbye, for the sake of homos' emotions who are at a glory hole with yellow buck teeth; who must be fleeing from purple summer in their crumpled soccer cleats. And cheers. (pp. 78–79)

Should we call this a teenager's unrequited gay love story? He is in love with his friend, but it is unclear whether the friend is straight or gay. On the other hand, the narrator, "I," seems to acknowledge his own sexuality to some extent. Attracted to his charming friend who plays soccer, "I" sucks his penis in an empty classroom on a rainy day. It is important to note what happens immediately after the friend ejaculates into the narrator's mouth: the friend who ejaculated "gave me a dry and lovely kick" and disappeared. Isn't the friend showing disgust toward "I"? Yet, the narrator calls it a "lovely kick." Moreover, only the wounded "I" says goodbye to his friend, "whisper[ing] like a wedding veil" . . . *I loved*

Dominguez, "We Asked People Why They Use Glory Holes. Boy, Did They Answer," *BuzzFeed News*, 10 July 2020, https://bit.ly/3LgAL03 (accessed March 22, 2022).—Ahn and Madhavan] *you so much. I can't hate you even though you are leaving me.* With that sentiment, the narrator becomes an abandoned "woman."

Then, there is sexual intercourse between men, in which masculinity and femininity coexist or vacillate with each moment. The prickly magnetism arises between a curiously confusing sense of beauty and transgression. Compared with straight love, gay love between teenagers becomes exponentially more complicated and burdened with layers of confusion and disgust toward one's own identity. There is also a sense of guilt and rage at the laws forced upon them by their surrounding world; self-pity; repeated self-harm; and anxiety that stems from being a minority that does not conform to this general law.

If queer material evokes problematic feelings in us, it will be because certain moments of their love are treated differently from that of straight couples. This may not be the case for those who are out to people outside of their community. But for those who are not openly gay—whether or not that is of their own volition—to love is, in and of itself, a minority rights movement and a journey in continued search of self-identity. And queer material, which takes shape through this process, gives straight people an opportunity to reflect on how ideological their ideas have been and urges them to mull over new ideas of humans, existence, and love. Due to his exceptionally gay sensitivity, the poetic speaker adopted by Kim Hyun is soundly trapped in the moment he is expelled from this paradise. After his love as a gay boy fails, the speaker becomes an "old baby homo" who had "shot a rocket beyond the boy's orbit before the countdown was over" (let's not forget that "homo" is a derogatory term). As such, the origin of this poetry collection is imbued with a profound alienation and melancholia that is nearly colorless.

The Bleak Landscape of the American Suburbs
and the Angel of Love

But this shouldn't be all there is to it. In Kim's poetry collection, the coming-of-age story of a gay teenager, as told by the poetic speaker, seems amplified in hindsight, as it resonates with incidents in his early childhood. Let's fast-forward to the future. From this point on, what I say is mere conjecture.

You may not remember this, but "Long-Tailed Darlin," the twenty-first poem of the collection, features a woman who has a tail. In some way, this narrative recalls an intersex person, member of a sexual minority. Since we are attending to a gay teenager's coming-of-age story now, let us take a close look at the following line: "The shortshortskylarks that saw Darlin's tail sang in chorus with mysterious skin." The fifth note in the poem, which glosses "mysterious skin," is a request: "The title of a film directed by Gregg Araki. I hope you apply velvet sound to the following narration from the tail section of the movie."

Mysterious Skin was directed by Gregg Araki and released in Korea in 2004. Through the repetition of never-ending loss and trauma, the film portrays how sexual assault ruins the lives of two children. What is difficult to explain is the behavior of a child named Neil (Joseph Gordon Levitt), who is forced into a sexual relationship with his male baseball coach. Once Neil becomes vaguely aware of his sexual orientation being different from that of other boys, his coach, who takes care of him and treats him with more affection than his father, becomes his object of affection. However, when this affection turns into a sexual relationship, it becomes an entirely different story. Filled with strange emotion, the child participates in the coach's "homosexual game" and even lures Eric, another boy of his age, to it. Through this, Neil fully brings forth his latent homosexuality.

As far as the coach is concerned, this incident is clearly sexual assault and child abuse that must be penalized. On the other hand, Neil remembers it to be the greatest excitement, and this is salacious and eccentric. Some may say that this movie is about the sexual assault of minors, not queerness. However, perhaps, precisely because of Neil's memory, the film has the characteristics of a queer movie.

Even as a teenager, Neil can't easily forget the coach and continues his life as a male prostitute. Can we call this "love" so readily? Common sense can be shattered and faith can be shaken. If our answer is "never," why *can't* it be called love? If not for the coach, would Neil be heterosexual? To what extent should we acknowledge Neil's self-determination? Or is it even something that can be acknowledged? The movie ends with Eric and Neil visiting the coach's old house on the sly and comforting each other. A narration is delivered in the last scene, as Neil apologizes to Eric; this is the quote referred to in the fifth note.

Sitting on the coach's old couch, the two lean against each other and spin, disappearing into a faint dot. This is accompanied by a line that goes like this: "I wished with all my heart that we could just . . . Leave this world behind. Rise like two angels in the night and magically . . . disappear." Is this not profound? The two wounded "angels" rise to the sky and disappear . . . Now, the two angels, who no longer have wings, feel like death is all they have left in life (We should pay particular attention to the part where Neil remembers the coach with a sense of loss and mutters, "You called me your fucking angel." This context surrounding the word "angel" does not appear in *Glory Hole*. Only those who have seen the movie would recognize it.)

~~I've gone on for far too long about this movie.~~ That is because in "Old Baby Homo," the first note is attached to the title, and, curiously, another note is attached to that note, specifically to "Min" (the name of the child "I" loved?). Moreover, "I thought of introducing songs that lent a hand to this note, but I decided to leave them in the dark. Except I've listened to John and Charles and Gregg and Min's 'the Origin of Love,' 'White Puppy Like a Beggar,' 'the Coach Violates Me,' and 'When You Were a Boy' . . ." is added to it.

It is not clear whether this is from a certain song or whether the poet, influenced by the movie, provided a fictitious narrative to the speaker's coming-of-age story and called it a "song." But this trivial "note on a note" seems to imply a critical moment embedded deeply in the speaker's memory. And here, we can create the speaker's coming-of-age fiction. This is to say, the poem somehow reminds us of the relationship between "two boys and one adult."

To sum up, there was an adult (the coach) who opened the boys' eyes to their gay identity, and there were two boys, one of whom abandoned the other over time. The abandoned boy was engulfed in the pain of old love and banished from paradise, hence left alone in a lonely and desolate world—this is what I wanted to say (this narrative can be completely rewritten; I encourage you to exercise your own creativity).

A coming-of-age story like this one will be a reference point to effectively bring readers closer to *Glory Hole* (or so I hope). Based on this, we can now coherently understand the following poems to a certain extent: "What Do Angels Do on Silent and Holy Night," "What Do Angels Do on Silent and Holy Night; Duane and Michals . . .," "The LA Angel" from "First of the Gang to Die," and "What Do Angels Do on Silent and Holy Night; Unfortunately for Dear Mr. Pale Blue Eyes." The two gay adolescents are transformed into the images of archangels Michael and Gabriel, which, in turn, appear directly or indirectly in the poems.

Michael returns home in the middle of the night and dreams of a flock of decapitated chickens fluttering their wings, and a cat named Gabriel licks and embraces the sleeping Michael; "Marilyn Monroe" takes off her clothes at home and is revealed to be a cross-dressing man, and her impending death is put on stage; the gangster and killer Hector briefly encounters James Franco, as if in a fantasy, through a glory hole adorned by angel's wings, and bleeds to death in a cheap motel; Michael, with his penis erect, enters a fantastical forest and whips Gabriel, and the two suck each other in the 69 position until the poem ends with them looking forlornly at the pale blue night . . . Aren't these variations on the same narrative, wherein two people in a homosexual relationship die in desolation after their paradise is lost? If you keep this in mind, you will have a much easier time understanding some of the other poems, too.

These two people were angels to other people when they were children, and they must have been angels to each other. In other words, the word "angel" and the various narratives surrounding it are tightly interlocked with one another, spiraling with deep sighs—for times of innocence, of being loved; for times of guiltlessly loving someone, and for distant times that you cannot return to; for times of violence and shame, and, at the same time, for memories that you can never shake off, for life that cannot fly off anywhere for broken wings. Therefore, these angels undoubtedly are the "angels of love." Without love, there would not have been all this pain.

Living as a Cyborg in a Sci-Fi Dystopia

Interestingly, as evidenced by the poet's notes, the backdrop of this collection is overlaid with the styles of many different photographers. As if inspired by Eric Hoffer, Gregory Crewdson stages and documents bleak and empty American suburbs like scenes from a Hollywood film; influenced by René Magritte, Duane Michals becomes known for sequence photography—all of these works overlap with Kim's poetry collection, bleakly and depressingly, eerily lonely, romantically and lyrically, and dreamily. It is a pity that I can only use words like these to describe their photographs. I recommend you look up their work on your smartphone.

Though the poet never explains this in his collection, those who have seen Duane Michals's *The Fallen Angel* might have a deeper understanding of the background in which the "angels" of this collection operate. In the work, eight black-and-white photographs are arranged in succession as such: Excited to see a woman in bed, an angel seizes her. He then loses his wings as if he is being punished and experiences human suffering. He finally runs out of the place, holding his coat closed. The setting, in which the angel loses his purity after sexual intercourse and degenerates into a human, is in line with the central hypothetical setting of this collection: a young boy opens his eyes to homosexuality and leads a happy life for a short time, only to be deserted in a lonely, desolate world to spend the rest of his life as if dead.

I think of gloomy city alleys littered with garbage. And a man wandering this city with sad eyes, his coat wrapped around him. Who would recognize him as an angel? In this respect, *Glory Hole* merges melancholy with romanticism. Notes like "A complete view of this concave tear can be found in Ryul's photo album *Terminal* (Ru, 1886)," in "Nine Years on Jupiter"; "Ashes of Time," which transplanted the sensitivity of the movie *Ashes of Time*; "Border," which dramatizes the midnight snow, daydreaming and love . . . all of these exhibit a romantic sensibility that calls to mind the works of Lee Byung-ryul and Park Jeong-dae. In this way, Kim pays homage to these senior poets through retailored notes and quotations.

And here is one more thing. Another fascinating world—an imaginary sci-fi dystopian world. A place where a gay teenager landed his spaceship after being forced out of boyhood. A place which could be figuratively called an "unfamiliar planet." Right here, conventional rhetoric makes for a persuasive background for the poetry collection. While there only are eight poems—"Galaxy Express 999," "Rewind," "Nine Years on Jupiter," "A Tribute to a Replicant about Which Gary Mumbled," "Greengrass Disappeared," "The Last Person on Space Ferris Wheel No. 12," "Montgomery Clift," and "Earth"—that take up a sci-fi theme in this collection; the others contain somewhat altered, contrary ideas like unfamiliar planets, time travel, space shuttles, UFOs, human clones and robots.

Of course, the sci-fi flavor of this collection does not highlight the developments of a brilliant scientific imagination, the creation of alternative histories, the dispersal of accurate knowledge or detailed storytelling. Rather, it is centered on themes taken from sci-fi writers such as Philip K. Dick—themes questioning where the boundary between humans and clones lies, as technology becomes more sophisticated; and, ultimately, where and how one can gain assurance of the certainty of human existence. Dick's novel *Do Androids Dream of Electric Sheep?* (which is altered and appears in the sixth note in "Greengrass Disappeared") is certainly an outstanding work of its kind, but the film *Blade Runner* (1982), which was based on the story, left an even stronger impression on me.

Anyone with even the slightest interest in cinema would remember the dystopian vibes of this film in a wink. It begins with the damp and dismal dystopian landscape of Los Angeles in 2019. Earth has long been devastated due to its exploding population and many humans have migrated to another planet. Replicants (human clones) have been created and mobilized to conquer other planets, but are easily discarded at the end of their four-year lifespan. While trying to eliminate the replicants who have made their way to Earth to extend their lifespans, Deckard (Harrison Ford) almost gets killed by Roy, the captain of the replicants. However, Roy dies alone and lets Deckard live, saying his final words in the rain. This continues to be an unforgettable scene for many: "I've seen things you people wouldn't believe. Attack ships on fire off the shoulder of Orion. I watched C-beams glitter in the dark near the Tannhäuser Gate. All those moments will be lost in time, like tears in rain. Time to die."

Is Roy really nothing more than a replicant? Is it fair to destroy him? Roy could kill the person (though some say Deckard is also a clone) who is trying to destroy him, yet he greets death without doing so. Is he not better than a human, at least at this moment? Is Roy's sorrow not sorrow? When Kim Hyun's poetry assumes the grammar of sci-fi, clones or cyborgs like Roy become poetic speakers, and they contemplate their existence with gravity. Furthermore, they ask us: *Am I human or not? If I am, why do I feel like I don't have a soul? If I'm not, why can't I be one? How much more human are you compared with me? Humans ravage Earth even at this moment, so what are humans* . . . If you too had a database like this, you would find Kim Hyun's sci-fi grammar even more convincing. However, there is another hurdle you must overcome.

Sirius dropped his underwear. The phallus of Tension Penis Corp. made a stiff appearance. Even the four beads under the glans looked just like mine. Had solitude a shape, wouldn't it be just like those beads? At last, I began tearing up my body with the old MacGyver knife that Sirius had handed me. [. . .] You too are nothing more than an industrial robot. [. . .] I lay on the bed with Sirius in my arms. I covered us with a blanket of emotions that have been banned since the twenty-second century. I closed my eyes. [. . .] *Joie de vivre*, which I never knew as a human, surged through me. But it might also be something stored in Fictions. I couldn't open my eyes. [. . .] Sirius, do you think I have a soul too? Code blue. Code blue. My lips twitched on their own. It seemed like an auto-destruct sequence had been initiated. [. . .] Where do you think we'll end up when

we die? asked Sirius. I can't forget it. I was reproduced with
a double-separated phallus from Tension Penis Corp. for
the coming generation. And looking for Sirius somewhere,
I've arrived here, on Planet 13, already. ("Sirius Somewhere,"
pp. 72–73)

Nothing is obvious. Who is "Sirius," who is "I," and where is
this unfolding? These are the confusions we encounter while
reading Kim's poems. And this particular poem, too, demands
readers to know its subtext in order to understand it. The first note
added to "Sirius"—"It is also the name of the first-generation pet
robot created by Olaf Sky, the founder of Tension Penis Corp, in col-
laboration with his lover, Stapledon Wolf"—only exacerbates our
confusion. Who is "Olaf Sky" and who is "Stapledon Wolf"?

The bottom line is that the poet is deliberately playing with "fake
notes" that pull apart the name of sci-fi author Olaf Stapledon.
Indeed, there is a novel by the name of *Sirius* in Olaf Stapledon's
oeuvre, and it is obvious that the poem took a cue from it.

In the novel, Sirius is a dog whose intelligence and sensitivity
are superior to that of humans. As such, Sirius is in a state of con-
stant conflict between dogs and humans—although the conflict is
consistently described in speculative terms. In any case, he has but
one human friend who understands him: a girl named Plaxy. They
grow up together, relying on each other, and once you know this set-
up, it is no longer difficult to identify how the poem altered this set-
ting. The poet borrowed the relationship between Sirius and Plaxy
from the novel and turned it into the relationship between Sirius
and "I," finally transforming this into a B-grade "queer sci-fi" story
where robots have exaggerated male genitalia.

If we connect this poem to our previous hypothesis, we can per-
haps come up with the following narrative. After experiencing some
kind of failure in love, a gay teenager is sadly awakened to his sex-
uality and is reproduced "with a double-separated phallus from Ten-
sion Penis Corp." He floats all over the universe like an angel who
has lost his wings. After wandering the planet, looking for his soul-
mate, he eventually comes across the one-of-a-kind Sirius, a robot
with "four beads" under his glans. The two then lie in bed and cover
up the "emotions that have been banned since the twenty-second
century." This must be a homosexual relationship (deep sorrow
aside, this kind of narrative also has a charm that is somehow both
infantile and narcissistic, and incredibly naive; think about "Tension
Penis Corp.!"—the sexual obsession and deification of male gen-
italia resemble the naivety of naked children who frolic together
because none of them care about one another's political inclination,
economic power or family background)!

From this point of view, *Glory Hole* is an oddly sad, bizarrely
entertaining sci-fi epic that narrates the tragic journey of a cyborg
who was born different from humans; who wanders the universe to
explore his identity and eventually returns to a devastated Earth to
greet death. "Inhumane," placed at the beginning of the collection,
is a secret invitation informing readers that the speaker of this
collection is not someone equipped with familiar human protocols;
although he is a cyborg, the speaker hopes to have a soul like a
human being. "The joys of life that I had never known as a human
surged forth. But this too may be what is stored in fiction." As we
can infer from this sentiment, the speaker faces multilayered
limitations—even if he admits that he's gay, he ends up doubting

the authenticity of the joy he feels. In other words, "being a cyborg was not my choice" is metaphorically echoing the confusion that being gay wasn't my choice. If "I" were a cyborg, there would have been someone who had created me, and I would only be something that feels, thinks and lives according to what's programmed. Why did the creator make me gay? "Who/what" made me and "who/what" am I? The questions, which gain gravity through sci-fi, are now met with porn stars and developed into metafiction.

A Metafiction Theater with Porn Stars

I pay you my respects for coming all the way here with me. An ordinary commentary would have been over by now, so it is admirable that you have endured this wall of text this far. Unfortunately (?), though, we still have a little way to go. My sincerest hope is that with the might of love you will read this text through to the end and come to love Kim Hyun's collection all the more.

Let me use slightly different words. Everyone knows that Haruki Murakami loves running marathons. So we wouldn't be surprised if he wrote about a character who regularly enjoyed running marathons and also suffered through the pain it caused. After all, he is a novelist. But, what if poet Choi Seung-ja wrote in the voice of a troubled speaker who enjoyed and suffered through marathons? People would no longer read her poems (of course, if Choi had enjoyed running marathons, she wouldn't be able to write in the voice of someone suffering in the first place). Because that is what it means to be a poet. Compared with other genres, poetry has a high ethical standard. And, indeed, poets have resisted depravity for

174

a long time due to their desire to equate themselves with their poetic speakers. For this reason, poets might be the first to pathologically accuse the world of depravity while establishing their own virtue. However, it is also undeniable that this innocent belief hindered poets from regenerating themselves and from expanding their imagination and the scope of their work.

In this respect, I think that the shift in focus of poetry from the 2000s—from poet to poetic speaker, then from poetic speaker to a type of role play—was an important transition that let us overcome the inherent limitations of poetry. Of course, its success and failure should be determined on a case-by-case basis. Nonetheless, it is clear that, by adopting this methodology, poets have attained some freedom to escape from the reality of their lives. In this more dramatized structure, they can let their imagination run almost like fiction.

Put differently, poets first attained the freedom to be depraved through role play. As poets became separated from their poetic speakers, they could let go of a little bit of ethical responsibility and become depraved through certain characters. In the case of Korea, the freedom to express decadence in poetry still does not seem acceptable. Therefore, poets who write such things have no choice but to turn to foreign countries as settings. The greater the depravity, the more outstanding the exotic background becomes. Only then can poets broaden the scope of their actions, while somewhat avoiding the arrow of criticism. Regardless of how realistic it is, the fact that the subject matter of poetry has expanded is a big change in itself.

I think there must be something inevitable in the fact that this young poet's first collection is set in the United States during the

1950s and 1960s, specifically in the back alleys of a metropolis or in a stark and dreary suburbia. If the poet's choice of speaker is considered deviant according to the commonsensical view, nothing but the world of dramatized fiction could effectively express his inner conflict and anguish. Therefore, poets in Korea who wish to fervently explore human decadence and demonic inner worlds through a character's depravity seem to prefer setting their works in foreign countries.

I have laid the foundation for talking about porn stars. This poetry collection introduces a powerful character, Linda Susan Boreman aka Linda Lovelace. She became widely known for her role in the hardcore pornographic film *Deep Throat* (1972). When this film was officially released in US theatres, it drew huge audiences and instantly turned Linda into a celebrity. People found the unabashedly shoddy film powerful; censorship by a repressive government that had declared a "war on porn" was also at stake. Hence, *Deep Throat* became a high-profile social issue, and it is still remembered as one of the most famous works of pornography in film history. Linda later confessed in her memoir that she was subjected to coercion and violence during the filming of the work, and joined the anti-porn movement. Linda's life was depicted in the film *Lovelace* (2013).

I don't know if you've watched *Deep Throat*, but there's nothing in it that we can really call a "plot." The most important scene is probably the one in which Linda Susan Boreman's face emphatically stays in close-up as she performs oral sex on a man. The scene is composed of a series of shots that are almost acrobatic; it makes the audience feel suffocated and causes them to wonder how such a thing could be possible in the first place. With this context in mind, it shouldn't be too hard to imagine how the following scene would've been conceived.

Susan arrived at Hank's thing. She raised her hands over her head. *Hank, I can't swallow this.* Susan was disappointed with Susan. *Only you can swallow this. Who else could swallow this if it weren't you? Susan, Susan, Susan,* Susan kept calling Susan out. *It's your retirement party today. It's time to show what a retirement party is.* [. . .] People surrounding Susan started to fall to death as if they were asleep. At that time, the Earth was at a power outage.

[. . .]

Susan swallowed till the end. All the fire crumbled. It was a refreshing early morning. [. . .] Susan floated into the bedroom, dragging a home dress with a discolored imitation pearl. Linda, barely stepping on the edge of Susan's clothes with her four feet, followed her in short and quick steps. During the long time when she was climbing up to her bedroom, Susan looked around at the faceless faces that chanted Susan. [. . .] *Susan! Susan! Susan! Where are you gone? Today's a retirement party for the Los Angeles Angel.* ("Susan Boreman's Retirement Party," pp. 140–41)

Queer, a novel by William S. Burroughs, who represents the Beat Generation and was a drug addict himself, contains the following line (The sixth poem of the collection, "Queer; the Story That Is Always Told," borrowed the setting of this novel): "Nobler, I thought, to die a man than live on, a sex monster." This is what Lee, the gay man in the novel, blurted out to his beloved young man, Allerton. The full passage goes as follows:

I thought of the painted, simpering female impersonators I had seen in a Baltimore nightclub. Could it be possible that I was one of those subhuman things? I walked the streets in a daze, like a man with a light concussion [. . .]. I might well have destroyed myself, ending an existence that seemed to offer nothing but grotesque misery and humili-ation. Nobler, I thought, to die a man than live on, a sex monster.[4]

Owing to societal pressure and often because of the lack of a supportive community or role models, self-hatred is common among gay people. In *Queer*, Lee is seized with loathing as he watches female impersonators, even though he is queer like them. Lee shares his memories of irrational self-hatred with Allerton. In this context, we can understand the fierce anger in *Glory Hole*—"you trashy homo" (from "Queer; a Story That Is Always Told"). As a result, we should imagine that the book is operating under the fol-lowing circuits of thoughts, though invisibly so: "I'm not a normal human. I wish I could accept myself, but I cannot. Then what am I? I'm rubbish . . ." When this mechanism of self-harm is translated into a philosophical question, it gives rise to a world of sci-fi and cyborgs. But if it is translated into destructive hatred, it turns into a world of porn stars. And if this happens relatively mildly, it becomes the world of a movie star who's living a fake life on stage.

I digress. Susan in the poem quoted earlier is clearly Linda Susan Boreman. Susan, in this set-up, sucks the genitalia of all the movie stars at her retirement party. When she finally reaches the

---

4 William S. Burroughs, *Queer* (New York: Penguin, 1985), p. 39.

genitals of the man named Hank, even she, the capable porn star, can't take it in. Under pressure that is disguised as praise, she ends up putting the penis in her mouth. It is violent and lonely. Linda Susan Boreman splits into Linda and Susan.

Should I call it a kind of pity, to watch Linda in her declining years, no longer in her heyday? "Lone Wood's Retirement Party," which is paired with "Susan Boreman's Retirement Party," similarly features a last party for Lone Wood, a retiring porn star. The party has an empty mood rather than a sensual one. "I should take a look at his monumental dick before I die. Try to get his foul temper triggered right now. Lonely people, only lonely people would understand my feeling tonight. Only lonely people would understand that this feeling is wrong," says Homo Dave Cummings. He sounds lonely, bleak and desolate. The same goes for Andy Warhol in "Blow Job." He feels a jumble of awful pleasure, disenchantment and emptiness, as if he were thinking, "I'm a sex monster, a subhuman monster. I can't stop indulging himself like a porn star . . . That's the person I am. That's what a human is."

Now Kim Hyun's poetic speaker is split into multiple states. In *Glory Hole*, he already appears as a "poet/writer/translator/poetic speaker/character." Yet, disillusionment with—and acceptance of—self-identity necessarily results in self-denial and split identities. When this becomes exacerbated, confusion arises within the character's once-consistent identity; and this is the moment where Kim's collection spontaneously joins a postmodern worldview.

"The Circular Ruins" is a short story written by Borges. It is the story of a man who creates a boy in his dream. The man doesn't know where he came from or how he came to be there; nonetheless, he arrives at an unfamiliar temple and, after two failures, creates a boy with the help of God. The man erases the boy's memory so that the boy will not come to realize that he is a creature made by the man's dream. He then sends the boy to another temple where he can glorify God. However, one day, the man hears a rumor that there is a charmed man who cannot be burned by fire. The charmed man was the boy he had made. The man was flustered because the boy, whom he had created with great effort, might realize his identity. At this point, we readers naturally separate the man and child as real and fake. But the story doesn't unfold in such a simple manner. The fire engulfs the temple where the man lives, and surprisingly, the man finds himself not burning. In other words, like his son, he may not be real and, instead, be a creature in someone else's dreams. This shattering of the presumed dichotomy leads us to metaphysical questions: Do we reality exist? On what grounds can we be certain that our existence, which we believe clearly exists, really exists?

The exploration of self-identity as queer existence, which is carried out through this volume, hence converges with the postmodern worldview. In the 1960s, Borges took the Anglo-American perspective on postmodernism and introduced various techniques; this had a huge impact on Korean literature in the early 1990s. In *Glory Hole*, among other things, Kim Hyun combines a methodology called "metafiction" with anxiety about one's own identity, and brings the latter back to life. If I were to explain metafiction concisely, it would be adding annotations to a fictitious text. Stories are nothing more than a fiction created by an author; the author may intervene and expose how the fiction was produced, thereby tearing down the boundary between the author and the reader, between fiction and reality. Our poet might have chosen this method of writing fiction as his method of writing poetry. Therefore, although this is a volume of poetry, it is more like a collection of stories—because the purpose of this book is to create fiction. Fake stories are created over and over. Notes extend beyond their boundaries, encompassing fake notes, fake citations, or notes mixed with facts and lies. And this becomes the primary format of this collection. It is a fiction, upon which another fiction is written, revealing that fiction is fiction, which is to unfold fiction . . . In other words, it's fiction/fiction/fiction/fiction/fiction . . . The poem "Regarding Cate Blanchett's Dream" is an example of this.

This poem draws on the name of real-life actress Cate Blanchett. In fact, in Jim Jarmusch's film *Coffee and Cigarettes* (2003), this charming actress played two roles—Cate Blanchett and Shelly, a world-famous movie star and a hippie woman, respectively. The two are cousins; they are congenial at first, but gradually show class contempt and jealousy toward each other. Blanchett also appears in a unique biographical film, *I'm Not There* (2007), where, in a sort of trans act, she plays the genius folk musician Bob Dylan.

It seems that our poet wrote "Regarding Cate Blanchett's Dream" by bringing bits and pieces of information to forge a new idea. The poem begins with a scene where "I" puts a dot on Cate Blanchett's face after looking at her picture at an outdoor cafe in Geneva. At one point, "I" becomes Cate Blanchett who is playing a role in a movie. At another point, "I" is texting with the person who put the dot on her face. The scene changes again and goes back to the past, and it feels like everything is happening in Cate Blanchett's dream. Which one is Cate Blanchett, and who is "I"? Is everything that is here "I"? When I stand between two mirrors facing each other, I am reflected countless times. Like this, Cate Blanchett proliferates, and later, the real and the fake become indistinguishable. Where is Cate Blanchett right now? Is the Cate Blanchett you are seeing really Cate Blanchett? If so, then whose voice were the notes to this poem written in? Are the real notes and the fake notes written by the same person or by different people? We comprehend their split voices as we enjoy the plethora of various characters in these poems; at the same time, we accept the stories that come into our view as if they are real. So what kind of pleasure and desire are we motivated by?

Now Then, Let Us Throw Away Our Fiction

Finally, we have arrived at the final chapter of this handbook to Kim's poetry collection. Let us give ourselves a round of applause. It would not be an exaggeration to say that we are companions at this point because we finished this book together. It was definitely not an easy book, but the more we understood it, the more it kept us intrigued. We still do not know the full extent of the database of subtexts working underneath.

If you look at "Earth," the last work of the collection, you will find the following note attached to the title: "One of the planets in the solar system; human beings lived there." Can humans survive on this pierced Earth? There is one last entity existing here. A streetlamp robot called "Blue Eye." Blue Eye looks all around, and eventually discovers that it is the last robot, the last existing entity, left on Earth. After going through a myriad of metafiction, it arrives here, only to realize that it is alone on Earth. So Blue Eye begins to dismantle itself in despair.

When the light of the Earth's last streetlamp goes out, a "flock of Transyl-white-butterfly-cabbage worms" swarms in and nibbles away at the Earth. Is this a sad scene? Perhaps yes, perhaps no. When the last existing entity on Earth disappears, this might be a sad ending for those who have empathy for Blue Eye. But for those who were keeping their eye on a "flock of Transyl-white-butterfly-cabbage worms" might feel differently about the ending—especially if they recall that the bisexual crossdresser Dr. Frank-N-Furter in the classic cult film *Rocky Horror Picture Show* (1975) came from the planet called "Transexual" in Transylvania. This last scene would be significant for anyone who remembers the movie's cult-like, kitschy playfulness and unrestrained charm.

In the final note of this poem, the caterpillar that had nibbled away at the withered planet pulls "transyl" out of its mouth, binds itself and becomes a pupa. A caterpillar giant enough to gnaw at the Earth! What splendid creature would this larva turn out to be after eating the withered earth? Could the Earth be a spectacular, cosmic, yet trivial butterfly? Can it be born again as an existence that is more free-spirited, boisterous, bizarre, but full of life? Precisely like transsexuals, who transcend the male–female dichotomy, so to speak. Looking at it this way, it's right to say that this book ends with the song of a jubilant diva who dreams of a happy ending in tears. Like ABBA's "Dancing Queen": "You are the dancing queen/ Young and sweet, only seventeen / Dancing queen, feel the beat from the tambourine, oh yeah / You can dance, you can jive, having the time of your life."

In this book, there is no familiar reality, but there is a reality that we have imagined through curiosity. Rather than disparaging this collection because it is based in subtext, if we were to evaluate its poems on how well they reflected reality *in spite* of being based in subtext, we would find Kim's *Glory Hole* sufficiently realistic. Moreover, if we focus on the charm and completeness of the story itself, we can appreciate his efforts as a whole. Kim's poetic speaker builds gay sensibility upon queer imagination and combines it with the conventions of science fiction and the methodology of metafiction. He is the founder of a new genre. Many people will talk about Kim Hyun for some time to come, and without him, the history of Korean poetry will not be complete. Welcome to the Queer Sci-Fi–Metafiction Theatre. The screening starts now.

Human⊙

the thirteenth angel that administers vitality
is silent and holy

at night
he spills ink

to give a pupil to a soul

over there, look at the distant hole,
a pupil approaching you

a heart's fate
is written with light

life is born
and ends with death.

the fourteenth angel
administers⊙